Vive la

A Frenchman's Perspective on American

Women, Love, Respect, and Relationships

GUY BLAISE

This book is dedicated to Anais, Cecile, Marie-Neige, Maxime and Nazaire.

La perseverance est la cle de la reussite car il est plus facile de renoncer que de perseverer." Papa! (Perseverance is the key to success because it is easier to give up than to persevere.)

ACKNOWLEDGEMENTS

I would like to thank all the strong, intelligent and beautiful women who have given me their support in writing this book.

To C. Hernandez, J. Kozaczek, S. Noel, K. Hartnett, A. Vaughan, A. Bailey, Dr Laurie, Nancy, H. Stevens, D. Roziewski, C. Davies, D. Hull, L. Allen, Colleen, Mary Anana, Ruthie, K. Lipsey, E. Bowles, Dr M. Taylor, Anne L. Afchain, Celine Piques, Frances, A. Trouve, M. Michallet, Dr M. Dayras and V. Gant. To all the feminist groups in Ile-de-France. Marcellin "Otis" of Bordeaux, Aurelien "Cems" of Greensboro, Nazaire Moupelo of Baltimore, Tonton Augustin Milondo and Joseph Kokolo in Paris.

Without the inspiration of my grandmother, Elizabeth, my center of gravity in Bordeaux, Mr and Mme Lorente in Port-Vendre, Lane in Charleston, Silvere in Lyon and Solange in Montigny les Cormeilles, this book could not have been possible.

Table of Contents

Introduction

"Tu peux rester coucher poursuivre tes rêves ou tu peux te lever pour les réaliser."

You can lie down to pursue your dreams, or you can get up to realize them.

As a Frenchman from the southeast of France, who has lived in America for the past 23 years, I've had the privilege of experiencing the culture of both countries. This has put me in a unique position to observe and analyze the differences and similarities among the women of France and America. And, as a man who was raised among five enlightened French aunts and who is now the father of four daughters, I am concerned by the way women are treated here *in the land of the free.*

I am not saying that French women have won the war against sexism and inequality, and some French women may not agree with me, but having left France and looking back from a different perspective, I can see how much they have accomplished.

Granted, they have not achieved all their goals towards emancipation and equal rights, but they are making great progress. I have spoken to many women in France and America about their relationships and their life experiences. What I have observed among too many American women is that the "princess" mindset - to meet Prince Charming and live happily ever after - is deeply ingrained and that some women will do everything possible to make that dream their reality. My goal is to not let my daughters adopt that mentality. I want them to pursue happiness and success. Whatever profession each of them chooses - doctor, mother, engineer, IT professional, or housewife - it should be because they want it, not because they feel obligated.

By writing this book, I hope to encourage women to reject the pressure placed on them to pursue a fairytale. I want women to allow their passions to take priority. If your career is your passion, do not apologize for not wanting to have children. If you prefer the company of younger men, do not apologize for your preference. If you ever find yourself in an abusive relationship, do not hesitate to get out. Follow your dreams and demand your equal rights as a woman. This is the attitude of French women that I would love to see more women in America embrace, including my own girls.

In this book I am sharing stories and lessons from women that I have spoken to, as well as my own thoughts. I will offer my honest observations from a French-male perspective. It is likely that I will upset a few men in the process. I may be called a snitch for breaking the guy-code, but I believe that American men have been comfortable in their own shoes for too long and being called a traitor to my gender is a small price to pay if my words motivate even one woman to raise her standards and demand the respect and honor she deserves. There simply must be a change in attitude towards women.

And this struggle should not be borne by women alone. I hope this book will encourage fathers of daughters in America to stand up and support women's rights and the causes that will elevate women. I believe the impetus exists to encourage men to support women to be educated and empowered, therein fighting sexism for the good of all. As a man who is aware of the challenges that women face in claiming their rights, I don't want to miss this opportunity to speak up and say very clearly that American women can find inspiration from French women to unite for a common goal.

Remember, you have a choice: *"Tu peux rester coucher poursuivre tes rêves ou tu peux te lever pour les réaliser."*

Chapter 1

American Man-Code

"Le paradis d'un imbecile est l'enfer d'un homme sage." French Proverb

The Paradise of a fool is the hell of a wise man.

My first experience and exposure to the American "man-code" – the implicit understanding between men that questionable actions, however sexist and misogynistic, can be condoned as long as they are kept secret between men - occurred many years ago when I was invited to a wedding. New to the country, it was explained to me that in American culture there is traditionally a "bachelor party" held the night before a wedding. I accepted the invitation for the bachelor party, not knowing what to expect. Thinking that I was going to a regular dancing club where alcohol is served and music is played, I received my strip-club "baptism."

I realized when I entered the club and was greeted by my friends that I had made a mistake by accepting the invitation. It was not a very "Catholic place" - a French expression for a place that lacks morality. I was sitting between the groom and his brother and at some point I learned that, for a few extra dollars, a male guest could disappear from the room and have sex with one of the dancers. I heard the groom's brother, a man in his thirties, say, "No, I go first!" and the groom responded, "I'm first, or we flip a coin." All the males at the table, about 15 in all, were having a great time and kept disappearing from the room. The groom and his brother had sex with the same woman that night and bragged about their sexual prowess. I was even more surprised to learn that the man-code was stronger than blood, because some of the men who participated in the evening's events were related to the bride.

I realized then, that education and morals are not necessarily related. The groom had a PhD in clinical psychology and the other had a master's degree in computer science. I made an excuse on the day of the wedding to not attend the ceremony and expressed my disappointment about missing the event to the newly married man a week later. I couldn't comprehend having sex with another woman the night before your wedding. He later explained to me that the bride may have had sex with a male exotic dancer at her bachelorette party as well. It was like building a house on sand. As of today, they are happily divorced.

The man-code demands that American men keep their emotional reactions in check, yet the display of emotions is the predominant social cue humans use in communication, both spoken and unspoken. American men are socialized to believe that it is not manly to show emotions, thereby continuing and compounding poor communication between the sexes. By contrast, French men are not shy about showing their emotions. Even tears of sadness.

This American man-code is also present in the workplace. Working long hours with male coworkers in America you hear constant and unfiltered conversations about women. Men often complain to their colleagues about their spouses and refer to women using offensive terms. I remember one colleague complaining that it was his wife's birthday, which meant she would want sex when he got home. He told us that Christmas, Valentine's Day, and her birthday were the days he had to please his wife in the bedroom. He made it sound like a chore or an inconvenience. To hear him tell it, they were intimate three times a year. This same man shared with us the location where his wife attended a class every Wednesday evening. Any man within listening range knew just where to find a presumably lonely and unhappy woman on any given Wednesday night.

I wondered if this negative attitude was shared among men because they believe it is what the others expect.

Are their lives at home happier than they would have their coworkers believe? I certainly hope so.

The man-code transcends race, age, religion, and cultures. Another workplace conversation overheard by many colleagues several years ago while I was working at IBM, was of a man who discovered that his wife was tracking his cell phone because she suspected he was having an affair. As a result, he began driving to a friend's house where he would drop off his phone before heading off to meet his mistress. The wife, believing that her husband was spending time with a male friend, was happy, and the husband bragged to his colleagues about how he had outsmarted his wife. Sadly, stories like these have been the norm that I have experienced while working with large groups of men in America. They are not told by all men, but by a good majority. I can also recall a male colleague saying that I "must be cursed" when I told him that I am the father of four girls. Imagine thinking that daughters are a curse! I do not claim to be perfect by any means, but I do know that I always have my daughters in mind when I hear men speak so terribly about women. It seems to me that French women tolerate much less sexism than American women.

If this is so, I want my daughters to adopt a French way of thinking when it comes to men. Such disrespect should never be tolerated. In fact, I would love to see all American women think more like the French, at least in that respect.

Finally, I can't overlook one of the latest man-code trends: the "red pill" theory. The term red pill comes from the American movie, The Matrix, where the protagonist Neo is given the choice between two pills: a blue pill to go back to his normal, unfulfilling life, or to take the red pill and learn the truth. In the red pill theory, as it applies to relationships, the "truth" is that men are naturally more dominant and are more rational than women and should trick women into getting what they want (to have sex and be served by women.) Proponents of this misogynistic movement believe that women don't really want respect and equality; according to the theory, they want male dominance and traditional gender roles to prevail in American culture. I cringe to think that women would buy into propaganda that says that a woman's key role is to procreate and please her man, and that men are not sexually attracted to intelligence.

Even more disturbing, married men who believe this rubbish may try to pretend to be more caring and loving towards their wives in order to get more sex.

As a future father-in-law, who will have only an opinion of and not a say in my daughters' choices of husbands, if they choose to marry, I am worried about what men my daughters will choose. The boys of today are the men of tomorrow. In present-day American society, few groups that teach boys the value of virtues still exist. Remember, honor is a virtue. Success and fame are prized, but they are not honor. The church, scouting, and military services have traditionally been the three institutions within American society that have instilled good values in boys and young men. Participation in all three are in decline, replaced by the false worship of money. I am doing my very best to teach my daughters what smart French women learn before investing their hearts in relationships. Love can bring us great happiness if we choose a partner wisely, but if we do not know how to manage it and if we are not with the right person, then we run the risk of suffering.

I hope that every American woman out there will understand my philosophy of love. To love is to give a person the power to destroy you and to trust that they will not do it.

Suffering in a relationship is not love, whether you are married or single and dating - that's what I tell my daughters. Before you say, "I do," test your heart and test your happiness. Choosing a husband should be like selecting a pair of shoes: you must like the shoes first, and then try them on and see if they fit. My hope is that after reading my philosophy and learning what French women know, you will raise your standard and be able to "read" the American man-code, counter its sexist mentality, and make chivalry one of your criteria when seeking a man to share your life with. While I agree that people should have some compatibilities in a relationship, it is not necessary to be a clone of each other to be happily married. *Voilà!* I hope this advice helps American women crack the "man-code" and refuse to be treated as less than equal by men in all aspects of their lives.

Warning: Men are willing to put women and themselves at risk to have unprotected sex, a practice that is irresponsible and dangerous. Women should never rely on a man to keep them protected.

Chapter 2

What American Men Say About Their Wives

"Tant que les animaux n'auront pas leur propres historiens, les chasseurs raconterons toujours leur gloire."

Until animals have their own historians, hunters will always tell their own glory.

If American women could transform themselves into coffee mugs and spend some time at their spouses' workplaces, the divorce rate in America would certainly increase. The cafeteria is the place where American men let down their guard and lose their loyalty to their wives. *Oh là, là*, if women could just hear them talk. It is the place where husbands complain to one another about what "she" did wrong.

I still remember a conversation between two work colleagues that I overheard years ago. One man asked another for advice on what to do about his wife's constant talking. He went on to say, "all she wants to do is talk about work and women's things the moment she gets home." The man sounded desperate for a solution. How do you tell your wife that you want her to shut up without hurting her feelings? He said he "just wants to sit down, watch TV, and relax at the end of the day, but his wife won't stop talking." Believe it or not, he had been married for less than two years. I have trouble comprehending a man who does not want his wife to share her day with him. Men seem to love everything a woman does while they are pursuing her but change their attitude when the chase is over. You can't help but notice the difference in these men when you run into them with their spouse. My, what a respectful and loving husband they become in the presence of others.

Would it surprise American women that some husbands, when they are around other men, accuse them of being gold diggers? Or that some complain about their wives gaining weight? Too often, the laughs among men are at the expense of their wives. A husband's loyalty to his wife must be unconditional. If he throws his wife under the bus when she is not present, he demeans her to the world. In contrast, in French culture there is a level of respect and privacy among couples. No matter what was said or done by the wife, her French husband has the decorum not to discuss it with other men. When discussing the past weekend, I have heard men say that they were dragged by their wives to the theater or a museum. Do American men believe that cultural events are "feminine" activities? Perhaps there is no disrespect intended here, but there is clearly a negative tone when husbands talk about their wives in the company of other men. A husband should never pass up an opportunity to elevate his wife.

I remember hearing Paul, one of the "stars" of the cafeteria who always had stories to share about his wife, say, "I always say to my wife, 'If you need something done, just say so.' She mows the lawn and then complains about doing it. It drives me crazy." A woman colleague responded by saying, "Why don't you notice what things need to be done and just do them?" Paul did not like her suggestion, nor that she did not find humor in his complaint, and that was the end of the conversation. Evidently, Paul's wife got tired of asking for his help and decided that she would have to do everything herself if she wanted it done. I am still unclear why his inability to help his wife with chores was something he was comfortable admitting.

I recall another colleague once making a joke about a time when his wife had gotten lost despite having a GPS in her car. According to him, "one day she was going to Georgia from North Carolina and she ended up in Virginia." This story earned him huge laughs and was followed by a wave of comments about women drivers.

I am sure that the women drivers being spoken about so negatively all have their own sides of the stories; unfortunately, men having lunch together in cafeterias will never hear them.

My general impression is that men reinforce their "manliness" when they are in each other's company. They tend to profess an attitude of us-versus-them. I have heard men say things such as, "be careful not to listen to her too much or you'll lose your freedom." When discussing a conflict, men feel the need to prove that "she was wrong, and I was right." Don't we all hope to be best friends with our spouse? What is the point of marrying a woman to become her enemy or her competition?

In my experience working with men and women in America, I have rarely heard women mock their husbands around their colleagues. Women tend to express their frustration with their husbands' actions or inactions, or sometimes of their children, but never resort to name calling, whereas men are comfortable degrading their wives for the sake of a laugh. Perhaps women filter their comments in my presence, but I seriously doubt it.

It is unwise and immature to denigrate a spouse in front of others. Any differences of opinions or frustrations should be addressed privately between the partners. American women do not hear the echoes of disrespect initiated by their husbands. In my eyes, a man who denigrates his wife in front of me is denigrating himself and shows a weakness in character.

A woman doesn't become miserable overnight. Men should look at themselves in the mirror first and ask themselves what role they played in her unhappiness. Women shouldn't blame themselves for their partners' boorishness.

Chapter 3

Subtle Harassment

"Si la femme ferme la porte, arrêtez de frapper dessus."

If a woman shuts the door, stop banging on it.

On a flight to San Francisco two years ago, I was seated near a window as others were boarding. Some people were trying to locate their seats while others were arranging luggage in the overhead compartments. There was a man in his early forties sitting quietly in front of me. The seat beside him remained empty. A few minutes before the pilot's announcements, a beautifully dressed and attractive blonde woman sat down next to the man. She settled into her seat and pulled out a book. Before she could open the book, the man asked her if she would prefer the window seat and added that he did not mind trading. "Sure, thank you," she responded. That was all it took. The man spoke about himself, his career, and his boat for nearly four hours, trapping her while the woman held on to her book, listened politely but wasn't engaged in the conversation. Overhearing the man promote himself, I was reminded of a French saying: "Les grands bavards ne sont jamais à court de mots" (big talkers never run out of words).

—

27

He elicited some obligatory laughs at his jokes from his captive audience, which I can only describe as "plaisir erotique" (auto-erotic pleasure) while the woman sat quietly and just listened.

His harassment was subtle, but clearly noticeable to anyone being observant. At one point, I even considered intervening. It is unclear to me why men don't always pick up on signals from women that say, "I'm not interested." They are either so self-absorbed in their chatter that they are oblivious to the signals or they are overly confident in their ability to make a woman like them. Neither of these is an acceptable reason to continue the harassment.

The other thing he did was to rattle off his skills. I have noticed that American men are very comfortable broadcasting their abilities and assets, even among other men. They blur the line between confidence and arrogance, becoming overly cocky about their accomplishments and intelligence. If they could, they would compete with the wind. It must take a lot of energy to constantly build themselves up that much.

Rather than allowing a woman to get to know him through his actions, he feels the need to announce his greatness. This strategy is a shortcut that requires the least amount of effort when attempting to make a connection with a woman. It is also a very simplistic way of trying to convince a woman that you are worthy of her time.

We say in French, *"Qui ne dit mot consent"* (to be silent is to consent). In reality, not every woman who is silent is offering consent. Sometimes the silence is a result of feeling intimidated or too uncomfortable to respond. After it happened, I thought about this experience on the airplane a lot and decided to share the story with my nieces in Paris and a few French women in my circle. They all agreed that type of harassment is common in France as well. Telling a woman to smile is another subtle form of harassment. A man would never suggest to another man that he should smile, so why does a man feel comfortable suggesting such a thing to a woman he does not know?

Maggie, an affable librarian at my daughter's high school, whom I have known for three years, shared an experience with me that happened to her. It began with subtle harassment and escalated into something more.

"I was living in New York City at age 21 and was new to the corporate world. Our department was primarily male, and I was the youngest in the group. One older male in particular often made subtle remarks about my appearance and how pretty I looked. Often times he would ever so slightly lick his lips when we made eye contact. Even with his inappropriate behavior, I never felt comfortable complaining to HR; I was the new kid on the block and was grateful for the job. After months of the same behavior, I found myself one day waiting for the elevator with a group of males. We all entered the elevator and turned around to face the doors. My harasser had been right behind me entering the elevator, which meant I was face to face with him when I turned. Three other men were standing and were silent. He made a comment about what he would do to me if only he could have 'his right here' and as he said the words, he extended his hand to grab me by the crotch. I moved backwards to avoid his reach, but there wasn't enough room for me to completely avoid contact. It took a long time to forget the sensation of his unwanted fingers against my pussy. I remember he laughed, as if his behavior was a harmless prank. I think the thing that hurt me the most was the reaction of the other men. No one said a word to correct him or to defend me.

Unlike the harasser, the other men had always been very kind to me; yet now they were pretending as if nothing was happening. My throat closed with humiliation. I couldn't speak up for myself, although internally I was screaming at the top of my lungs. It's frustrating to look back on the experience today because I should have handled it very differently. If I could go back and do it all again, he would have felt his own crotch being touched, but with the heel of my boot."

I strongly believe that men should change their attitude towards women. I also believe that men must condemn bad behavior by other men that they witness. When it comes to men harassing women in front of other men, silence by male witnesses equals consent to carry on with these actions. Injustice against women is a human injustice and should be fought by all humans.

Chapter 4

Sexism and Chivalry

"L'amitié ne demande rien en retour que d'être respectée dans le role privilégié qu'est l'amitié."
Friendship requires nothing in return but to be respected in the privileged role of friendship.

I learned a lesson about American-style chivalry when I was still new to the country. I invited two women colleagues to a restaurant for lunch and paid for their meals. The women viewed my paying as extraordinary and, after returning from lunch, they told our colleagues that I had "treated" them. Our male colleagues began to smirk and asked me, as soon as the women were out of earshot, which one of them I wanted to sleep with.

When I told the men that I viewed paying the bill as merely a kind gesture, they joked about it, saying that I was a fool for spending the money if I wasn't interested in pursuing them sexually. I have since been told that when a man takes a woman to a restaurant and pays the bill, he wants to sleep with her. *Non, non.* My intention was never to have a ménage à trois with them, nor to sleep with either of them. In addition, I would never get involved in a relationship with a colleague.

In France, when a man takes a woman out to dinner, he pays the bill. It is not considered a "treat"; it is expected, and most French men and women know it. Chivalry, in France, is not toxic to women and doesn't stigmatize them as weak. Nor should it be interpreted as assuming that a woman is unable to take care herself. Whether a woman is French or American, a chivalrous man reveres her femininity and expresses chivalry by willingly giving with his heart.

Living in America, I am often puzzled by the bill-paying guessing game played by dating couples. There can be a level of anxiousness experienced by a woman, brought on by the American cultural understanding that a man has expectations of sex if he is paying the bill for a meal. This can cause a moment of awkwardness experienced by both a man and a woman when the bill arrives, an uneasiness that could easily be remedied if Americans would come to expect that the male companion should always foot the bill. Women must be clear and in control of their sexuality first, so that they feel comfortable communicating that they are not bartering food for sex in accepting an approach from a man. That mentality is so ingrained in American men that they need to be told up front that trading food for sex is not an essential element of romance.

Independent women are often wrongly blamed by insecure men for killing chivalry when, in fact, their attitude about being treated has been cultivated by unwanted advances from men who view paying the bill as an "investment or entitlement" for sex. On the other hand, men of principle understand that it is about respect and reassurances, not about buying sex. A true gentleman will take care of the bill, even if his female companion is a millionaire. My belief is that having a man to pick up the tab should be the norm across the board and a "thank you for dinner" is more than enough thanks for this gesture. Of course, there is nothing wrong with a woman paying from time to time if she invites the man out while they are in a relationship. In general, French men see women paying the bill at a restaurant as a dishonor. But a couple in harmony wouldn't question who will pay. Whatever arrangement they agree upon, is acceptable.

I have heard tales from American women where men have "conveniently forgotten their wallet" or been asked to "take care of the tip" when the bill arrives. This seems bizarre to me and not a good way to begin a relationship. I believe, if a man is incapable of fully treating a woman to dinner, he is also demonstrating his inability to financially contribute to a relationship. This will put a woman in a position of uncertainty.

What I have observed in both France and America is that women think ahead and consider all possible outcomes in order to be well prepared. They show up to a date prepared to pay just in case things do not go according to plan. For a Frenchman, taking a friend or a lover to a restaurant is like giving a gift to a friend: there is personal satisfaction in making a friend or lover feel valued.

I must admit to my annoyance when I see a couple walking into a restaurant, giving the impression of being very connected, then see them sharing the bill at the end of their meal. I do not believe in equality between men and women in everything we do in society. We shouldn't always measure ourselves to women in the name of monetary equality. We can be different and still be equal in rights.

In France, men get anxious at the look on the waitress's face when their date pulls out her credit card. For French men, paying at a restaurant is a rite of seduction. We often act quickly to pick up the bill and then smile discretely, glad that the bank card went through without being declined. I find it shocking when men make arguments for paying for a meal based on ideas such as "If I invite her, then I will pay," "I won't pay if she is a colleague," and "I won't pay if she invites me." I do validate men who will allow the woman to treat from time to time, when she insists that it is important to her, usually as a way to show her appreciation. Her doing so is a way to make her mind be at peace and releases the pressure of owing too much. There is no danger of emasculation. Chivalry is a form of elegance and class. Yes, I am for equality between men and women, but let's not change the code of love and respect. Traditions should not change because of modernity or because more women are working. Some men use the excuse of equality to be stingy. Chivalry is part of what we call in French *savoir vivre* - to know how to live.

A woman is like a flower, it takes a great gardener to make her bloom. Preserve your heart and soul for the best gardener. French women seek men who are caring; American women should seek the same.

Chapter 5

Honesty and Lies: Traps of Online Dating

"Il ne faut jamais croire aux belles paroles, mieux vaut croire aux belles preuves."

We must never believe in beautiful words, better to believe the beautiful proof.

I grew up with the idea that churches were the best place to meet one's "perfect" partner because church is a place where people who share the same religious beliefs and values gather. In my own family, my uncle met his wife at church two decades ago. I find the same situation in America, where churches often have programs for singles to connect.

Because American churches are dying, and attendance at church services is waning, online dating is becoming the new "church" for meeting mates. I have met many women who have been active on dating sites for years and have never successfully met their ideal man. I think of these women and online dating sites as birds and trees: no matter how high and far the birds fly, they come back to land on the tree.

Many women that I have met have tried dating sites off and on and experience chronic disappointment. They find

—

their hopes being cut short, and many are the victims of men's lies and men who view online dating as a sport, like fishing.

Women tell me that men engaged in online dating frequently embellish their status and their salary to look powerful and financially stable. In their minds, power equates to sex. I have noticed that American women complain more than French women when it comes to men lying about their appearance. American women tell me they have met many guys that do not look the same in person as they do online; their profiles often have photos of themselves that are distorted in their favor or from when they were younger. I've been told that the most common lie men tell is about their height. Maybe American men are afraid of being like Napoleon!

Perhaps this is more common in America because of the pressure in American society to look a certain way. Appearances seem to hold more value in the United States. I can only speculate. Finding love via the Internet is difficult in a sexualized society such as America. Women go online with the intention of finding someone for a long-term relationship but tend to jump in too quickly. In my opinion, women who become sexually involved with a man too soon are likely to be dumped. Men tend not to value something that they can get too easily. At the same time, men will play along with the idea of finding a relationship when they are truly only interested in sex. They lie about their intentions, knowing that most women are seeking a commitment. I am not a specialist in men's psychology, but I observe more similarities between French and American men. There are men out there who are opportunistic predators, ready and willing to exploit an available woman for sex. Women who take their time to know a man before becoming sexually involved will know if the man is there for sex only or for the long term. My message to American women is to follow the philosophy of many French women: treat all men on dating sites like a rosebush. A man who has beautiful words without actions is like a rosebush that doesn't produce roses. Trust is earned when promises are kept.

An honest person, French or American, tells the truth despite how that truth will be received. However, stretching the truth on occasion is inevitable in relationships. Lies are tools used to attain something, or to get away with something, or simply to spare feelings. A woman may lie and say that "the sex was great" to avoid hurting her partner's feelings or ego. Lies can be told with good intentions in an effort to keep the peace in the relationship. I am not suggesting people should lie to their partners, but I understand the reasons why sometimes people choose to do so.

To women suffering in silence, no matter the source of your pain: Know that resilience is the key to rebounding. It's okay to be afraid. Do not give up hope. Please keep your head up and continue the journey ahead. Above all else, never give yourself permission to lose hope.

Chapter 6

A Letter to a Newly Wed American Man

"Les meilleurs mariages se font entre pareils."

The best marriages are between equals.

A colleague of mine came to me two weeks after his wedding and asked me for advice for a successful marriage from an "old man." I wrote him this letter to relay one man's advice on success in marriage. I am sharing this letter to explain my philosophy of a good marriage. I welcome American fathers to adapt it for their new sons-in-law.

Dear Robert,

Congratulations on your wedding and thank you for sharing the pictures of you and your beautiful wife. And welcome to the club of married couples! You asked for the secret to a happy marriage, and I can tell you there is no magic formula. But I can tell you this: marriage is comprised of hard work, with a dose of good luck. Based on what you shared with me prior to your wedding, both of you came from different levels of education. To make your marriage work, you must respect your partner's background and remember that you have much to learn from each other.

As your colleague, I have often called you a "fine American young man" because of your manners and your attitude. I rarely saw you in a bad mood and this quality will serve you well in your marriage. Keep that good humor! Your mother and father raised you well, but you alone are responsible for your character. You have learned from the three schools in life: home, academics, and street. All three have shaped your character. Use that good character to treat your wife right. You will earn her respect and trust by being respectful and trustworthy. Don't expect anything from her if you don't deliver it consistently yourself. American men are notorious for embracing male privilege, at least in the eyes of this French man. Remember, Robert, being nice and doing something nice for your wife won't make you lose your masculinity. Au contraire! Tenderness is a virtue.

Don't let finances create an environment of tension. Your wife should be involved in all financial decisions, and you need to decide together how you wish to handle purchases, savings, and financial management. Just keep those discussions out of the bedroom. Financial equality creates a strong and healthy foundation and is critical to your relationship. Women have enough trouble being underpaid in the workplace; in marriage, equal rights should prevail.

Never be afraid to admit a mistake or apologize for unintended hurt. Humility is a great quality and is a sign of strength, not a weakness as American men are sometimes led to believe. If you are always right and she is always wrong, you've got a problem! If you give her a smile when you are wrong, you will definitely earn her heart. We say in French an admission of guilt is forgiven. It is okay to say I was wrong, stupid, and I am sorry. You will not lose your virility, trust me!

Laughter is an anti-depressant. Make time to enjoy a peaceful evening at home watching your favorite comedian. Like we say in French, *"Qui sème le rire récolte la gaieté"* (he who seeds laughter harvests joy).

Every woman on this earth knows that most men have trouble expressing their feelings, primarily due to the perception that showing your feelings is not manly. You might call them "sexually impaired," meaning marked by their inability to communicate and interact with their partners, both inside and outside of their bedroom.

I am not shy about discussing sex with you. Make love to your wife, a lot. Sex is in the headfirst. Romance shouldn't be only for the French. A bouquet of flowers to her is a great start, but flowers don't talk. Not sharing feelings and emotions is like starving a plant of water. Tell her how you feel with tenderness and you will melt her heart.

Chapter 7

Equal Pay for Equal Work: A Human Right

"Promouvoir l'égalité entre l'homme et la femme
est a la fois un devoir politique et moral." –
French President Emmanuel Macron
Promoting equality between men and women is
a political and moral duty.

In his first speech to the nation after his election, French President Macron declared equality between women and men to be a "great national cause." By the end of the first year of his presidency, progress was being made towards closing the gap in pay between men and women with the same qualifications doing the same job. President Macron sent a clear message to end the injustice against women.

According to the French agency INSEE, the pay gap between genders in France in the private sector is at 6.8%, meaning that women earn, on average, 93 percent of what men earn, an all-time low[1]. The French government has created an equal pay index for which companies are required to report gender pay-gap information. Companies failing to do so are penalized. Much of this change can be attributed to

French feminist groups who have put pressure on the government to make equal pay for equal work a priority.

In contrast, the American gender pay gap was closer to 20-25% among all workers in 2018, according to the U.S. Census Bureau. In other words, women were making 75 to 80% of men's pay for the same work.[2]

More than 50 years after the Equal Pay Act was adopted in the U.S., the pay structure still reflects an obsolete belief that men have a more important role in society. I applaud the lawmakers who passed this law in 1963, but I question the sincerity of a government that does not enforce a law that would benefit women.

Nine administrations have come and gone since the early 1960s, and American women are still discriminated against in the workplace and in pay. How can men in power who are fathers of daughters justify their inaction to enforce a law that would benefit not just their daughters, but all American women? I hear so many promises for equal pay, but little action. *"La promesse est une dette"* (a promise made is a promise due.), as we say in French. I have also observed first-hand the lack of women in higher executive positions in America.

Women in America now hold about 27% of corporate board positions, according to data from ISS Analytics[3]. A study in 2018 showed that when it comes to women and minorities occupied in this area, France made great progress by passing a law in 2011 that became effective in 2017, "Loi Cope-Zimmerman" which requires corporate boards to be comprised of at least forty percent women[4]. Men tend to fight to preserve their positions of power, privilege, and domination. I have observed the aggressive attitude of American men when negotiating their pay or asking for a pay raise. At the same time, American women, who often perform better than men and produce quality work, are reluctant to ask for more pay.

Women in America should negotiate harder for increased salaries. In 2017, Asian Americans were among the highest paid women in the U.S[5]., largely because they tend to have better education and work in lucrative high-tech jobs, but perhaps they also negotiate harder for higher pay. American men must change the misogynistic ideas that women must be grateful for what they have and stop trying to negotiate their pay or ask for a raise.

I'm concerned that the fracture in the women's movement in America is holding them back. Women need to speak as women first, not as liberals versus conservatives. By unifying, they can overcome the male domination that is pervasive in politics as well as in the workplace. Women who unite will have a stronger voice to be heard by the federal government and lawmakers. Like the French, American women shouldn't be afraid to strike and join protests to demand equal pay for equal work. To fight and win this battle of equal pay, you must expect resistance and criticism from men who want to "defender leur bifteck" (defend their steak, or in other words, defend their privileged positions). To misogynistic men in America I would say that equal pay for women does not mean less pay for you. Equal pay is a human right.

P.S. French women could not have gained all the rights they have in France without the cooperation of men. American women should not alienate men, but instead recruit them. Men are also brothers, husbands, and fathers.

[1]Elise Coudin, Sophie Maillard, Maxime To- Family, Firms and the Gender Wage Gap_INSEE, July 2018.

[2]Institute for Women's Policy Research September 2019; www.iwpr.org

[3]Jena McGregor, "After years of "glacial' change, women now hold more than 1 in 4 corporate board seats" Washington Post, July 2019

[4] www.egalite-femme-hommes.gouv.fr

[5]US Board of Labor Statistics, August 2018

Chapter 8

Eleven Tips for American Women from their French Counterparts

From conversations with my French women friends I have compiled this list of 11 tips for American women about relationships:

1. A relationship should never be a game of power; it should be a partnership, regardless of salary or background.

2. Jealousy is not a sign of love, but of insecurity.

3. Keep your vulnerability in check and make a man earn your attention. Value yourself first, then let the man value you.

4. Don't waste your time being a "helicopter" partner, constantly worrying about and checking on your man – you have more important things to do.

5. Never show your man that you love him more than he loves you. He'll take advantage of you and he will think he can get away with anything.

6. Preserve your unique, personal "brand" and don't let go of your individuality. Recognize that one couple can have two identities and say no to blind submission if your man asks you to assimilate into his life.

7. Always keep a mysterious side of yourself. Resist the urge to overshare to a lover.

8. There is no need to refer to your previous lovers—the past is the past. Knowing about your past partners triggers a man's insecurities.

9. Do not stay in a relationship that does not bring positivity to your life.

10. A man should not blame his affair on the "other woman." Whether or not she knew he was already in a relationship, he knew.

11. Your needs are as important as your man's. Don't be afraid to speak up and assert your needs.

Chapter 9

Who's Cleaning the House?

"La premiere égalité, c'est l'équité." – *Victor Hugo*

The first equality is equity.

Universally, if all domestic work being done by women was remunerated, women would be making more money than men. Even though French women are earning more degrees and working, they still do more domestic work than French men and play a major role in raising children. I thought things would be better in America because it is a younger nation compared to France; however, that is not true. I often hear from American male friends: "My wife asked me to do this or that." When a partner waits to be asked to do something that benefits the family, it is akin to exploitation. What he's implying is, "If I am not asked, then it is her responsibility to do it."

According to the French agency of Statistics, Statista, almost 50% of married French men can cook, which could make a huge difference for French women and alleviate some of their stress. But 58% of women are still cooking and only 17% of men cook (E. Moyou-Statista 26

Nov.2019). One of the criteria for French women looking for a potential husband should also be his ability to clean, wash dishes, iron, and fold clothes.

Same-sex relationships seem to be more egalitarian in domestic chores.[1] In the last fifteen years, men in France have improved and are doing more for their children's education changing their attitude from "helping her" or "doing her a favor" to "doing their share" as fathers and spouses (Titiou Lecoq Slate.fr 16 Oct 16). It is not necessarily for them to show their good intentions; French men are facing strong and confident women who have higher expectations. The results are that married men with an egalitarian attitude have a better relationship with their spouse and tend to live longer than single men (Titiou Lecoq Slate.fr 16 Oct 16). They also stay longer in their relationships (Brian Ogolsky University of Illinois, Daily Mail news 2014).

What I have noticed in America is that some women often wear a "veil of happiness" in public, while enduring the weight of chores at home; even more so when there is a baby in the family. This is not fair at all. I cannot comprehend the mindset of men bragging about earning more money than their spouse and earning the "right" to help less at home. Most French women wouldn't tolerate doing domestic chores while their partners watch soccer on TV, regardless of how much money he makes. Many American and French men need to be told of domestic tasks because they have no idea what their partners do. Some were raised like princes and everything was given or done for them; they never learned how to do the laundry or take out the trash.

A woman may need a clean house to keep her sanity while the man may not share the same sense of urgency.

The danger that I see among American women, especially those with conservative values who seem to accept "the man rules the roost" style of family management, is that they tend to underestimate the challenges of motherhood in combination with being responsible for the majority of household-upkeep responsibilities. It is simply a ticking time bomb. Unhappiness and resentment are sure to follow.

My advice for American women who are unhappy with the unequal distribution of responsibility on the home front is to look at their French counterparts. Identify the tasks first and propose to the man what he is comfortable with. Get rid of the stereotypes of mowing the lawn being a "man's job" and doing the laundry as a "woman's job."

Think about what will work best for you and your spouse based on your strengths and interests. The goal is to feel like a team without keeping score!

Couples who share the responsibilities of child raising will feel more engaged, less stressed, and ultimately will be setting a positive example for their children. As we all know, the boys and girls of today are the husbands and wives of tomorrow.

You may need to remind your partner that pitching in to take on domestic chores is not doing you a favor - it is a shared responsibility. In the end, communication is imperative. If you don't feel comfortable having those difficult conversations, write your spouse a letter.

Don't let frustration build up and destroy a good relationship. It is unacceptable for American women to lose their identity and self-esteem because of housework burnout. When couples work together, *Vive la Différence.*

Equality within relationships starts by sharing kisses and then by sharing the household responsibilities.
Like we say in French, "*Au cimetière nous sommes tous égaux.*"

In the graveyard we are all equal.
[1](Matthieu Maurer 18h39.fr 22 Juin 2018).

Chapter 10

Older Men with Younger Women

"Le cœur a ses raisons que la raison ignore." –
Blaise Pascal

The heart has its reasons that reason ignores.

Often, when a young woman marries an older man, she is immediately accused of not truly loving her spouse and marrying him only for money. The couple sometimes becomes the subject of speculation and gossip. As a result, sometimes these women must make the tough decision to walk away from loved ones who have trouble accepting their unconventional relationship. This happens both in France and in America. I see feelings and connections between two people like the relationship between a key and a door. Whether the key is old or new if it fits it opens the door.

Women who choose mature men may certainly be looking for security and stability, but that isn't necessarily the only thing they seek. For example, there is Aida, a young French woman I know from Montpellier who married a man 14 years older than her. Aida said, "I chose him because I needed someone who could listen, and he knows how to love me." There are certainly mature men - young at heart and dynamic - who make wonderful partners to younger women.

—

Kristen, a transfer from New Jersey now living in North Carolina, is 18 years younger than her husband. She told me, "I found tranquility after I met my husband. I dated men my own age and they were so immature. I felt like I was raising a child."

Many young women that I have spoken to complain about the level of immaturity among men their own age. A mature man finds his youth in a young woman and it benefits him because he stays in shape to keep her. Love has its own formulas that we don't necessarily understand. The laws of attraction can be stronger than age difference. Mature men tend to know what they want after having some experience, whereas young men are having trouble figuring out life itself.

A woman who marries an older man because she sees him as *papa-gâteau* (sugar daddy) marries for the wrong reasons.

Unfortunately, sometimes an older man will divorce his wife, a woman his own age and the mother of his children, to seek a younger woman, holding onto a naïve illusion that a younger partner will magically stop his biological aging.

And, sadly, some men are attracted to younger women because of the proliferation of online pornography, which often uses younger women and leads men to fantasize about them.

To women in America, I would say that there is no such thing as the perfect relationship in the eyes of society. From the outside looking in, people find it easy to criticize a relationship that is not their own. Always follow your heart and choose what is right for you, not what society wants for you. Do not ignore a man who shows you love, protects you, and gives you stability in this stormy life, a man who uses his words to communicate and not his fists. It doesn't matter if he is 77 and you are 30; as long as he is the missing piece to your puzzle, the opinion of others should not be relevant.

Chapter 11

Love and Sexuality Made in France

"La jalousie provient d'un manque de confiance envers soi-même."

Jealousy stems from a lack of self-confidence.

Are the French better lovers than Americans? *Oh là là*, how often I get asked this! It is quite a difficult and multi-layered task to compare. I will say that French lovers do not separate sexuality and love. The French are simply more comfortable with nudity, sexuality, and public displays of affection. For example, in France there are estimated to be 150 nudist beaches, as well the Piscine (swimming pool) Roger Le Gall where urban naturists are welcomed. In contrast, a surprising number of Americans seem to be uncomfortable seeing women's nipples exposed, whether during swimming or breastfeeding. French people don't have those hang-ups.

There is an obvious contradiction here: Americans are generally uncomfortable with public nudity while simultaneously leading the world in porn production (Peter Nowak, Canadian Business magazine 2012). French people do not put labels on anything sexual. Public displays of affection are part of the culture. French women are sexualized by choice.

Ultimately, they make it clear to everyone that they control their bodies. French culture does not shame or make people feel dirty for expressing their sexuality. We do not have a switch to turn sexuality on/off when it is deemed appropriate. There is a universal mystique surrounding French lovers, which has been cultivated by an openness that supports expressions of love, where a person's overt sexuality is not considered risqué or taboo. In America, sexuality is most often perceived as lewd or inappropriate.

Another notable contrast between the two cultures is how the French deal openly with prostitution, while Americans keep it under wraps. While prostitution is illegal in France, it is an activity acknowledged and tolerated by French authorities; prostitutes pay taxes and are registered for social security. In her 1983 book *Regards sur les Francaises* (*A Look at French Women*), Michèle Sarde, a French author, reveals that French prostitutes earn more and are more successful than other European prostitutes. Many men don't hesitate to approach sex workers in public parks such as the Bois de Boulogne in Paris, even though prostitution is illegal. France has always maintained its reputation of being a country of seduction and forbidden pleasures, sexuality being one of its tourist attractions.

Finally, I would argue that churches in France have limited influence on people and religion does not define sexuality, compared to the influence of the church in regions of America. Although 65% of the population of France is Catholic, France is also one of the most secular countries in Europe. In parts of the U.S., particularly in the South, the church largely defines sexuality. I am aware of life in the southern U.S. "Bible Belt" states where church and state laws are connected. Outside of the Bible Belt, one encounters more people open to different forms of spirituality.

Many Americans choose Paris as a marriage-proposal destination because it is considered by many to be "the most romantic city in the world." I often hear negative anecdotes of the French by American men for surrendering to the Germans in six weeks in 1940. American men like to remind us of the liberation of France from German occupation as a means of diminishing the Frenchmen's image. It may sound amusing, but it also confirms that French are truly lovers and not fighters. It is clearly a form of propaganda and chauvinism of American men to tarnish the image of the country that American women elevate in their souls.

Sex is only meaningful when a woman can connect with a man mentally and emotionally. A good lover builds chemistry by hitting that intellectual G-spot. A man who does not want to take the time to connect with his partner is like someone wanting to enjoy a beautiful day with his eyes closed. What is the point?

However resilient, women are also like flowers: soft and delicate. Love making is not war. It is an art form. A man does not always have to be aggressive in bed to please a woman. Learning to know her personality, her body and her needs are the key to passion in the bedroom.

Chapter 12

Women Who Love Women

"L'amour est le meilleur medicament contre la haine."

Love is the best painkiller against intolerance.

Last year, while walking in the streets of Le Marais, known today by Parisians as the gay district of Paris, I had a revelation: the most tolerant people that I know, both in America and in France, are gay. Despite living in a world where homophobia is the norm, my gay friends are the ones who open their hearts and minds to all and see differences as something to celebrate.

In America, there seems to be more emphasis on the differences in people, including their sexuality, compared to France. It continues to surprise me how, in a country of immigrants, the "them versus us" mentality is more prevalent than ever. After living in America for two decades, I sadly catch myself many times in a room counting people by race, gender, handicap, age, or sexuality. I'm ashamed to admit that I have adapted the American mentality of categorizing people based on skin color or orientation.

Have you ever caught yourself observing a lesbian couple and pretending that you are open-minded? The truth is you are analyzing their every move and gesture to know who plays the male role and who is more feminine. Or you might find yourself judging why such a beautiful girl would choose this lifestyle. Observing humankind has helped me to realize my own ignorance.

I realize that lesbian couples are not exact copies of heterosexual couples. Assigning traditional gender roles to a couple of the same sex is like eating with chopsticks and wondering which stick is the fork and which is the spoon. I also realize that the word "choice" is not appropriate because it implies that sexual orientation is not determined at birth. It would be no different than someone asking me "when I chose to be straight." Lesbians don't play the hetero by using an arsenal of sex toys. Like a friend of mine put it, "Only a woman understands another woman's sexual needs."

Behind the faces of these women are the stories of their resurrections and how they transitioned from secrecy to opening up to their families, friends and colleagues at work. A coming out is an act of bravery with so many unpredictable consequences; it is a rebirth.

Women who love women are discriminated against based on their sexual orientation. African American women who are lesbians have a triple struggle being at once female, black, and lesbian. Some women would rather live in secrecy than face the judgment of the outside world. Do you blame them? Their philosophy is to live their truth in secrecy.

Homophobia is a form of racism. Lesbianism is not an illness and attitudes are evolving. In many churches, homosexuality is still a sin. A man who has been left by a woman following her "coming out" will usually accept this fate better than being left for another man. Men's egos would rather have it that way.

My conversations with gay women suggest that coming out for a French woman is not any different than coming out for an American woman. Lesbian movements in France are on the rise and slowly winning battles against prejudice. And yet gays and lesbians are still suffocated by the Catholic Church. The statistics in France speak loudly of their challenges: more than 17,000 suicide attempts and an estimated 200 deaths a year. This is a high rate for a community estimated to be about 4% of the French population.

To learn more about the church's stand on gays, I reached out to Father Xavier, an Episcopal priest in America with decades of experience counseling married couples, both heterosexual and homosexual. He said, "I see marriage like the relationship between monks and God. When 25 men live together and decide to sacrifice their lives to serve God, it is a commitment." He looked at me and asked, "Do you think that men living together for 30 years don't have problems? They do and they find a way to resolve them to live in peace. I see marriage the same way. Marriage is the constant discovery of the person that you married, and a couple have to talk to solve differences and to have peace."

I asked him what he thought of gay marriage and the LGBTQ community. Father Xavier said, "The Episcopal Church is in favor of gay marriage. We accept everyone. We even have women priests." I asked if he believed in an egalitarian marriage like we see happening in France right now. Father Xavier said, "That's the type of marriage we would hope brings respect between spouses. I think heterosexuals have a lot to learn from people in same-sex relationships." I must admit I was eager to hear his explanation. He said, "People in same-sex relationships care more for each other at a level that would embarrass heterosexuals. That's true love. I am not saying that they don't have differences, but they find a way to resolve them."

As things are changing in France and people are seeing the positive side of same-sex marriages, I hope that

Americans will embrace the same level of tolerance and see that we have much to learn from each other.

Chapter 13

Mental and Emotional G-Spots: Why French Men Attract

"La langue est un organe dont on se sert occasionallement pour parler."

Boris Vian

The tongue is an organ that is occasionally used for speaking.

Despite the idea promulgated in America that French people are fussy and stuck up, I still notice a lot of appreciation for the French by Americans. Why do American women like French men? Is it the accent alone or is there something different about the French that American men do not have?

Definitely, American women view French as the language of love. I have been caught off guard many times by American women asking me to repeat ordinary words such as "potato" or "butterfly" (I struggle saying those words in English) or to say "*je ne sais quoi!*" aloud. The famous line "*Voulez-vous coucher avec moi, ce soir?*," from the 1974 hit song "Lady Marmalade" by American singer Patti Labelle, is still on the lips of American women today. Many women have asked me the meaning with big smiles on their faces.

My friend Jean Claude and I agree that differences between French and American culture are greater than similarities regarding a man approaching a lady and courting. Jean Claude, who has lived in America for 15 years and owns a French bakery, puts it like this: "We don't make a case to a woman based on the size of our manhood. French men are not on the top of the penis-size charts in Europe, despite our reputation for being womanizers, but we have the words and the charm. Size is relative." Penis size might be extremely important to some women while others are more interested in "how the ship maneuvers in the ocean," so to speak. One thing among men that is universal is that we are obsessed with our "magic wands," also known in France as *les baguettes magiques.*

Jean Claude added, "What is this obsession with many dates at different restaurants during courtship? Food is not the only place to express love. Museums and public parks are also romantic places. *Oh, mon Dieu!*"

French men will establish an emotional connection with a woman before anything physical. We will romance her with flowers or poetry. A French man will pursue a woman with passion. We will show our intentions through thoughtful expressions of admiration. French men love to sweep a woman off her feet, and we are quite comfortable with public displays of affection. For the French, giving a first kiss is the beginning of a relationship. As Jean Claude's euphemistically says, "We don't wait for the trumpet to sound to claim a woman after the first kiss and show to the world that she is taken."

I suggest that another element of attraction for Frenchmen is our openness towards different cultures. I don't know anyone in France who has never traveled outside of the country. We travel throughout Europe and often speak many languages. The more you travel, the more you embrace others.

I have been asked many times by Karen, an American woman, for advice on the best wine to buy for dinner or how to pronounce a French word in a recipe, despite the fact that I am a bad cook and my culinary repertoire consists of a French omelet. (No, not all French men are great cooks, despite the reputation of French chefs and French cuisine.)

For American women, France is Paris. It is the ideal place for a romantic proposal, the perfect destination for a wedding or honeymoon. Although there are many other beautiful places in France, they are less often seen by Americans.

My advice to American women is to broaden your horizons, literally. There are so many interesting and beautiful places to visit besides the Caribbean islands and other tourist destinations, including Paris. France has much to offer beyond the Avenue des Champs-Élysées.

Chapter 14

Before You Say "I Do"

"Il n'y a qu'un bonheur dans la vie, c'est d'aimer et d'etre aimer." – George Sand

There is only one happiness in life, to love and to be loved.

There is nothing wrong with learning about divorce before you get married. No one enters marriage with the intention to divorce, but it is wise to educate yourself with the sometimes-painful truth of reality. Know where you would stand if your marriage were to end. My own experience with divorce taught me that valuable lesson.

According to its Census Bureau, the U.S. has a divorce rate estimated at about 50%, a rate that is increasing. In France, the divorce rate is slightly higher, with 55 out of every 100 marriages ending in divorce (Statista-statistics 2016). Every potential bride in America should ask herself why the divorce rate is so high and understand the main reasons that people split. A woman or a man shouldn't jump in the "pool" called marriage without knowing the depth of it. Although it takes two to make a marriage, in both the U.S. and France women initiate divorces about 70% of the time.

Marriage is a serious decision and commitment. Unfortunately, relationships do not have a "mountain," the top from which someone can see the future. A smart woman should never decide who her life partner will be while she is "madly in love," but wait until the passion and craziness settles down. The old saying "love is blind" is true. Only a fool tests the depth of the water with both feet.

There are no supporting statistics to say that knowing someone for many years before marriage will guarantee a longer marriage. What I'm seeing in America is that many people marry their high school sweethearts only to become different people a few years later. The promise by a future husband of a great life together is just a promise until it is a reality. Remain lucid in your thoughts. As we say in French, *"Ne jetez pas votre parapluie quand il fait beau"* (do not throw away your umbrella while the weather is fine).

Know yourself before getting to know someone else: where you came from, how you were raised, the values you were taught. Reflect on these things before choosing a person to be your partner. Like we say in French, *"Si tu ne sais pas d'où tu vas, sait aumoins d'où tu viens"* (if you don't know where you're going, at least know where you came from).

—

Before you say, "I do," know that marriage is not always joyous. You never fully know someone until you live with them. Dating is a period of unrealistic best-behavior that cannot last indefinitely. Above all, your partner's character should complement your own. You should be able to lean on your partner during challenging times. A couple must have the same vision for a marriage to work. Marriage in France is more of a partnership where lovers remain individualistic. American women could benefit from a similar mindset.

Before you say, "I do," consider how much you really know about him, his choices, and his way of making decisions. Do you know if he believes in love? There are men who marry because traditions say that after reaching a certain age, a man should have a wife. Others are hopeless romantics who genuinely seek their soulmate. How does he feel about sharing domestic tasks and having children? When choosing your future husband, don't just look at the man, look at how he interacts with his mother and sisters. How he treats the female members of his family may reflect how he treats all women.

How does he handle money? In general, when a French wife handles household finances, money tends to be managed conservatively. They think of tomorrow. Some American families enjoy spending frivolously, and many men are guilty of overspending on symbols of success such as expensive cars and watches. What would be your financial predicament if things went sour in your marriage? We say in French, *"Dieu gouverne au ciel, l'argent gouverne sur terre"* (God is the king in heaven, and money is the king on earth). No matter how strong you believe your relationship is, if your husband is the bread winner, you are vulnerable. Better to be a wife with a Plan B than an estranged wife with no resources. If you are a stay-at-home mom, think about tomorrow in your spending. Many young men live with the illusion that they can just be "a little bit faithful" or "a little bit in a relationship."

Therefore, my message to a woman thinking about marrying a guy because he is so handsome, cute, tall, or funny is do not put unlimited power into his hands. You have to be your own police. There are some young men who think they can be a little bit mature but who refuse to grow up. They stay active in social media and video gaming groups and refuse to pick up their phone when their girlfriend calls or put down their electronics, because these things seem more important than the value of their relationship.

A marriage without a solid foundation is like a bird without wings: it will never take off. A young woman who is seeking a husband should think like some French women: judge a man by his interest in you, rather than by all the other topics he goes on about. In life, you need to be his most important topic.

Not all men are "marriage material." French women are realists about it. Being a nice guy doesn't automatically make you relationship material. We say in French, *"L'habit ne fait pas le moine"* (wearing monk's clothing doesn't make someone a monk). Before you say, "I do," don't allow your lover to bring you flowers only when he's in trouble or on Valentine's Day. Flowers should be an expression of love, not bribery for forgiveness. By the same token, gifts do not always have to be expensive. A thoughtful gift can be the most valued.

Some women have had multiple breakups with the same man, but they keep going back to him expecting different results each time. Multiple breakups mean you are repeating the same mistakes; changing your actions may give you different results. Life's mistakes are a part of the learning experience. Educate yourself. Know who you are and what you want out of a relationship. When things do not work out, it is not a fatality. If you don't fail, you will never succeed. Like we say in French, "*La différence entre l'échec et le succès c'est la patience*" (the difference between failing and succeeding is patience).

Life is too short to stress over a man who doesn't deserve you. Peace starts by respecting your inner self. Like we say in French, "*La vie est belle*" (life is beautiful). I would advise against keeping communication with former lovers and passing them off as "just friends." Being 100% committed to your relationship means not keeping strings of attachment with your past. Loyalty is not a weakness. Men are like watermelons, as we say in France. They are hard to pick, and you should probably touch a few before deciding on one.

Chapter 15

A Conversation with Colonel Chadick, MD

"Dans une grande âme tout est grand." – Blaise Pascal

In a great mind everything is great.

I met Colonel Chadick through a local Francophile club that helps Americans improve their French. Throughout his military career, he has traveled around the world and worked in military combat zones as a medical doctor. Colonel Chadick met his dynamic wife, Irene, a native of the city of Rouen in Normandy, when he was stationed in France. As of this writing, they have been married for 26 years.

After meeting Colonel Chadick and his wife many times, I asked if I could interview him because, to me, he exemplifies an American man who transformed his own chauvinistic attitude towards women into an egalitarian outlook, thanks to his French wife.

Colonel Chadick shows his affection for his wife freely and doesn't apologize for holding her hand, unloading the car, and carrying the groceries. I am always impressed by his native-sounding French and his ability to change seamlessly between speaking English and French.

Q: *Bonjour, Colonel. How are you?*

A: Ça va très bien. Merci!

Q: *How and why do you have such an interest in the French language and the French culture?*

A: I grew up in a family that loved languages and travel. My mother was a French teacher in high school. My father was a major in the United States Army. I embarked on a military career and I met my wife in Normandy.

Q: *Why a French wife and not an American wife? How does it work for you, the differences in culture?*

A: Love is unpredictable. I would say that it's my destiny. I think a difference in cultures keeps our communication alive. We always have things to talk about, even after 26 years of marriage.

Q: *Would you marry her again?*

A: (Smiles) Yes, I would definitely marry her again. She keeps me straight and I am a better person today because of her.

Q: *What does she do that American woman might not do?*

A: She keeps me away from that American male mentality and chauvinism. I am not saying I don't have buddies; I am just selective of who I hang out with. As a white American male who has traveled and seen other cultures, I know that a man in America, especially a white man, can't hold himself up as moral pillar of society when he is busy doing so many immoral things.

Q: *That's a bit harsh.*

A: Oh, believe me, I have seen some horrific behavior in the military. Rape, sexual assault, physical battery, harassment, you name it. What happens in the military is simply a reflection of our larger society.

Q: *Be more specific, Colonel.*

A: I had to change my attitude towards women decades ago. I have a wife who is a partner for life that I love and respect. My wife belongs to a woman's gardening club, and let me tell you, sometimes there are stories that she brings home from married girlfriends that are depressing, such as domestic violence, verbal abuse, and denigrating treatment from their partners.

Q: *Are you referring to American women in marriage or relationships?*

A: Invite four American women - married or single and in a relationship - for coffee and ask them to discuss the nice things their partners do for them. You will see. My wife often asks them, and they struggle to name three.

Q: *Based on your experience of practicing medicine, can you share one case that hits your conscience?*

A: (Pauses) I have hundreds of stories. I had a case of Miss X who was beaten up by her fiancé because he found contraceptives in her handbag. She may have realized that she made a mistake by accepting a ring from him and she wasn't ready to have a child with him. She told me, "He doesn't like condoms." Clearly there are men out there who don't know that condoms are not just contraceptives; they are also a prevention of sexually transmitted diseases. I have another case, Miss Y, who came to see me, alarmed, at Naval Medical Center Camp Lejeune because she had had sex with a guy who "never liked condoms" but presented her with his blood-test results. She realized that she never looked to see if it was current or if it was even real. Just to tell you that we live in such a selfish society that people will choose their sexual gratification over their safety.

Q: *It is only the man's fault? If things are bad in a relationship, why not leave?*

A: Most women think, "He is better than no man" and "Better a bad man and bad sex than to be alone." There is a defeatist mentality among women. When I travel back from Europe, it is much more noticeable to me.

Q: *Are you saying that chivalry is dead in America?*

A: I don't even know it existed in the first place. I don't know if Americans truly understand what chivalry means. It is ambiguous and we don't know how to apply it to modern life. I was a product of an American society who saw women as second-class citizens, until I met Irene.

Q: *Sounds to me that you are shifting more from American male-code attitude to a more egalitarian attitude. What is happening inside your heart?*

A: The white American men birth-right attitude needs to change.

—

Chapter 16

Sexually Frustrated Wives

"Le sexe est le baromètre des sentiments." –

Yann Moix

Sex is the barometer of feelings.

There is a problem in the bedroom of American couples. Sex is all about him first, rarely about her. Most women that I've met are extremely frustrated by the lack of intimacy in their relationships or having to work harder in bed to please him. What I am hearing is that many men have the attitude of "Come, satisfy me" and their mindset, 80% of the time is, "How can she please me?" I have realized while listening to American women that if men are asked to choose between making love to their wives/partners or receiving a blow job, most men will choose the blow job as it requires less work on their part. Sex is therefore a selfish act for many men. They don't care to ask a woman what she needs or desires in bed.

I often think about the attitude of American women towards sex and how complicated it is. I also think about the impact of the Puritans' ideas in America and how, for a long time, women didn't ask for anything in bed; they simply accepted what they were given.

I met Monica, a fifty-year-old pharmacist, at the local YMCA. She had been married for 25 years and she confided in me that she couldn't take a sexless marriage anymore. She told me with a strong Southern accent, "It does take two to make things work in a relationship. I finally realized after years of trying different ideas that I am not responsible for the whole thing by myself. I am open, willing to communicate and willing to do anything it takes, but seriously... I've been hurt a lot that way by making myself available or trying something new and being rejected again. I finally decided that's enough. I can't beat myself up this way anymore. As soon as I yelled at myself, it was like a veil lifted and I decided to focus on myself and my own happiness."

Michelle, a nurse married for 10 years, sees her husband as "allergic to work and too lazy to work harder in bed." She added, "That attitude is prevalent."

Despite the changes occurring in America, where women are more and more vocal in denouncing the injustices done to them, I still see American women stuck in the mud so to speak, unable to free themselves from the mindset that women should be obedient and put their own sexual needs after their spouses'. French women will not wait *pour la tombe de neige* (for the snow to fall) to be outspoken about their sexual displeasure. Here in America, particularly in the South, it seems religious conservatism carries over into the home life and influences relationships.

When asked how much of their time in bed is spent pleasing their partner, most American women I interviewed said 90% to 100%, meaning women are doing most of the pleasing. I am still stunned by this. I am not promoting the stereotype of a French lover who will sweep a woman off her feet. Lousy lovers can be found in the country of romance, too. But in general, for the French, love is about sharing moments of pleasing each other. At least that's the mindset.

I realize that, according to many women, the image of the perfect couple seen in public is an illusion. Men may pretend to care about their wife in public, showing other men what they've got and how successful they are in their "possession" of a woman. In reality, inside the house and in the bedroom, men care less about their spouses and their feelings.

What I am hearing is that women hate it when their husband's attitude changes after they marry. Many men have an attitude of "I got you, I put a ring on your finger, and I don't have to do anything else anymore." This leads to bitterness, and in some cases, women give up on dating men entirely. I've heard so many times the defeatist mentality "It is what it is," and it upsets me. I realize that many women are lonely, and that loneliness is why frustrated wives live vicariously through films, TV shows, and romance novels. I also notice that some women barely talk about these things with each other, including their best friends. Why would they? They're all in the same boat together. Others, fortunately, are more comfortable opening up to their friends.

Monica told me, "Why talk about things that are already understood by other women?" adding, "If you both agree that a banana is yellow, there is no need to have a long conversation about why the banana is yellow."

Of course, my reaction at first was, "Why not talk about sexual discontent with your spouse?" Most women agree that it's not the easiest topic to bring up in discussion with a spouse. It opens them up to vulnerability, and even humiliation.

Michelle commented with bitterness, "When a woman is undressed and used by a selfish lover, she loses her glory."

Sexual discontent is sometimes experienced prior to marriage by American women and yet, they enter marriage with the hope that things will get better, which I see as absurd. In France, sexual compatibility is one of the major factors in choosing a spouse. Few men or women would willingly enter a marriage without sexual compatibility. In most cases in France, if the sex doesn't click, there is no relationship. Listening to these women I wondered, if the divorce rate in America is 50%, then of the 50% of couples who remain married, what percentage are happily married with a satisfying sex life and what percentage are sexless or sexually frustrated? I wonder how many women prefer to be happily married in a sexless marriage with a partner that they can tolerate than be unhappily married with a great sex partner that they despise.

I am aware that a couple's sex life may decrease after years of marriage, regardless of the country. You may be surprised to hear that some French women are completely happy in a sexless marriage. The difference between French and American women is that French women are open and honest about their attitudes towards sex. French women are comfortable talking with their spouse about sexual issues while American women seem terrified to broach the subject.

Are they afraid of hurting their spouse's feelings, or are they trying to preserve some sort of artificial harmony?

An opinion survey of 1,007 French women by the French magazine ELLE/Ifop titled "Ou est la vie sexuelle des femmes en 2019?"(where is the sex life of women in 2019?) revealed that 31% of women are not satisfied with their sex lives and another 20% see sex as a spousal duty that is not necessarily enjoyable. This survey also found that 65% of French women surveyed are okay with being in a sexless relationship (Etude Ifop pour ELLE realisee du 28-29 Jan 2019). So, American women are not alone; there are frustrated French women as well. The French find different ways to deal with their sexual frustration, however. Some French women will seek a divorce if they are not sexually satisfied in their marriages or they will become involved in an affair. I believe that French women are less afraid of the stigma of being divorced. It is about their general attitude towards sexuality.

What many American men do not value is the sense of togetherness that constitutes a couple. Being married and being selfish is like wearing pants without a belt. I strongly believe that women are the belts that hold up our pants. Americans say, "happy wife, happy life" and in France we say, *"La femme est la plus grande richesse de la famille"* (the biggest wealth of a home is the wife). Sex does not start and end in bed; sex is about courting your wife every day, from January 1 to December 31. Love doesn't take a holiday. Women should be courted every day.

My observation of American men has been that too many of them are not aware that they are lacking in the bedroom. They have convinced themselves that they are a woman's greatest gift. The many men that I have spoken to are very proud of their sexual abilities in bed. Some have even used the word phenomenal, and yet none of that is consistent with what their wives are saying.

I surprised a friend of mine with my response when she asked me how I keep on point, sexually speaking. I told her I spend my free time on French YouTube watching women's videos/sex shows in which women talk. Any intelligent man knows that we must make the effort to listen to women if we want to become better lovers. It is like going to the gym consistently to build strength. I keep up with topics relevant to women and I make an effort to see things from their perspective.

The French government does not restrict the freedom of communication related to topics about sex. I find it absurd that in America, the FCC (Federal Communications Commission) makes it legal to teach you how to load/use an assault rifle but illegal to teach techniques on making love on YouTube. I'm amazed at the number of American commercials for erectile dysfunction that promise a satisfying sex life for both partners, implying a strong erection is the solution to all sexual problems. If American men do not make the time or put in the effort to stay physically and emotionally connected with their wives, a pill alone will not solve the problem. Reading relevant magazines and books that focus on women's issues is a way of keeping that connection.

I am going to point out to all the American women in this situation that you are not responsible for the selfishness of your partner. Here's my advice to American men:

American men will be better lovers when they understand that the purpose of love making is not to reach an orgasm. Instead, men should imagine love making like a chameleon traveling: it is a slow journey that takes time to reach the destination. During the trip, the chameleon adapts to each environment (by asking her needs/wants) and making stops along the way. What matters for women is the journey, not the destination. The longer the trip, the better it is.

An American man will be a better lover when he understands that it is okay to let their woman take control in bed if the woman is willing to do so. I know for sure that some women love to be dominated, while others do not; it is all about communication.

No man should be ashamed to *"branler sa queue"* ("to fiddle with the tail" or masturbate) discreetly prior to love making to extend the love making with their partner. Like we say in French, *"Tous les moyens sont bons pour atteindre ses objectifs"* (all means are good to achieve the ends). Sex toys to spice up the relationship are fine if both partners are engaged. But sex toys used by women alone to compensate for the men's deficits will not solve the problem. Sex toys can't kiss.

A great lover is a man who is kind to you, to his associates, and to a stranger. Kindness is an honorable quality, not a weakness.

Chapter 17

Men Who Cheat

"La plus belle preuve d'amour est la fidélité."

The best proof of love is fidelity.

Writing this chapter, my intention is not to tell American women how to handle a cheating spouse; I am simply making observations about French and American culture. The idea that French women tolerate cheating is false. In fact, French women are probably less tolerant than American women when it comes to spousal infidelity. What is probably the biggest difference between France and America is the way an affair is handled. Many Americans think of an affair as a biblical sin that brings condemnation, while the French don't involve religion in their affairs.

It is not uncommon for French couples to lay their cards out on the table and come to an understanding that works for both partners regarding an affair. Other times, both partners are having affairs and choose the "don't ask, don't tell" policy. Couples in France do get divorced for cheating, but not all French men are cheaters.

True, there are men who are serial cheaters, jumping on anything that moves and never admitting to being unfaithful. Like we say in French, "Un ivrogne n'admettra jamais qu'il est ivre." (a drunk will never admit he is a drunk.). There are no statistics available to support the claim that most French men cheat. The well-respected French agency Ifop notes in a survey titled "Les Francaises et l'infidelite feminine a l'heure des sites de rencontres," (French women and female infidelity in the age of dating sites), that more and more French women are cheating on their men, but the gap is still huge. One of the main reasons for cheating among both genders is the lack of intimacy or sexual satisfaction. Cheating among highly educated couples is more common than among the less educated. Married women who are financially independent tend to cheat more (Ifop.com 2017).

This suggests that there is a connection between cheating and social economic success. Perhaps a woman that can take care of herself financially, if she is caught having an affair, is more willing to take the risk. A woman who is completely dependent on her husband for support has a lot more to lose if she is caught cheating. The lengths that some men will go to when they are determined to cheat on their partners are surprising. If your partner wants to cheat, they will find a way to make it happen. Spying on your spouse is exhausting and never works. Some people are willing to forgive infidelity and work on rebuilding trust within the relationship. I make no judgments here. No one knows you better than yourself. If you know that you can't forgive your partner, the best thing to do for everyone involved is to end the relationship and move on. Peace of mind is priceless.

One of the first concerns of an American woman when courted by a French man is often the stereotype of French men as womanizers, cheating on their partners. I can't speak on behalf of all French men, but I will say that what is morally wrong in the Anglo-Saxon puritanical view is not necessarily wrong for the French. An affair is an affair and I cannot condemn or support someone's individual decision. We say in French, *"Le coeur a ses raisons que la raison ignore."* (the heart acts in ways we cannot understand).

Men tend to justify their cheating by placing blame on their spouse. They might say, "She isn't the same person she was when we met" or "She let herself go." There seems to be no thought given to *why* the partner is behaving differently. Is he treating her differently? Are his expectations of her reasonable or unreasonable? Is he making sure she feels appreciated? Loved? Are they communicating their concerns with one another? Sometimes men cheat to be with the opposite of their spouse. If the spouse is thin, they cheat with someone overweight. If the spouse is too strong emotionally, men seek a more passive mistress. At the risk of making a generalization, French women are notorious for being, as they say in America, high maintenance. French women are often strong-willed and demanding. An affair for a French man can sometimes be a brief escape from his critical wife into the arms of a nonjudgmental mistress.

Like in any misogynistic society, women cheaters are harshly condemned. Sadly, some women, both American and French, blame themselves exclusively for their husband's affairs.

Regardless of the many faithful French husbands that exist, I do not believe that we will ever shake off our reputation for being romantics, players, good lovers, and/or cheaters. "*La reputation c'est comme le lait – la nuit comme le jour il reste blanc*" (reputation is like milk – even in the night, it remains white). The reputation of French men will never change.

The argument that there is always a woman out there willing to sleep with your husband is another false claim made by men designed to add pressure to a woman and have her cave into his intentions. Cheating is a choice, not a given.

Chapter 18

A Conversation with a Deacon's Ex-wife

"Si le mariage est le prix que les hommes paient pour avoir des relations sexuelles, le sexe est le prix que les femmes paient pour se marier." – *French proverb*

If marriage is the price men pay to have sex, then sex is the price women pay to get married.

As I was pursuing my education in the United States a decade ago, I had the opportunity to listen to groups of Christian American men and women on college campuses. I realized that there are young people who strongly believe in having no sex before marriage. I was curious to ask how they could abstain in a society that bombards them with sexual content: in movies, television, songs, and even billboards along the highways. Is only coitus forbidden in the Bible? Is oral sex not considered sex? Why do Americans tend to associate sex with religion?

To explore these questions, I decided to contact Marge, a longtime friend and the ex-wife of a Baptist deacon. She met her then-husband when he was doing his training with campus ministry while she was a student of psychology. Their later divorce sheds light on the issues being examined. Driving to Grand Rapids, Michigan, to meet her, many thoughts were running through my mind. Why did she want to tell her story? I had a moment of hesitation, but I decided to go for a frank conversation with her. After meeting at a quiet restaurant, we sat down to talk openly.

Q: *How did you resist the temptations of sex in college?*
A: We followed strict dating rules when we moved to Phoenix, Arizona, so we were almost never alone. We did some serious making out, but we never had sex.

Q: *How hard it is to live together as virgins and share a bed?*
A: I lived with his family for maybe a couple of weeks then moved in with a couple of girls. But I don't remember us ever feeling or giving in to temptation when I was there. We never shared a bed.

Q: *What happened after you got married? Your husband must have been hungry and like we say in French, made love to you like a rabbit.*
A: Having sex after marriage had always been a chore for him. That's why it surprised me so much that my ex-husband

was so uninterested in it after we married. No oral sex from him to me. I went down on him one time and it wasn't my choice. He pushed my head down on him, which may be why, after that, I never thought of or wanted to do that with him again. It was a bad memory. He forced me to go down on him, which shocked me. I felt like he was using me, taking from me.

Q: *Did you have high sexual expectations after years of abstinence?*

A: I don't really like to think about my disappointment about the lack of sex in my marriage. I'm just so thankful I didn't have to face the rest of my life in a sexless marriage.

Q: *How can you be so unhappy sexually and stay in a marriage? A French woman in your shoes would have left.*

A: I just kept waiting and hoping that someday things would change. I seriously thought about separating but couldn't figure out how to make that work logistically.

Q: *Why not seek professional marriage counseling to talk about your issues? Due to religious concerns, at what point was divorce an option?*

A: Twice I asked for help from the church. My ex-husband was very good at keeping others at a distance and not being open to self-examination or change. Though church elders tried to intervene, it was unsuccessful.

Q: *Why would you trust men within the church to fix your problem? They may have been doing the same thing to their spouses.*

A: I wrote a letter describing my dysfunctional relationship with my ex-husband to the elders, so they'd know what our marriage was really like and to prepare them for my going public, as I felt I needed to do.

Q: *Did you have the opportunity to talk with your husband first?*

A: I did. On many occasions, my ex-husband said he didn't want to discuss our sexual issues. Then I met with the elders and they reassured me that they supported me in my decision to reach out to them. One of the elders told me there were several times when he could see my ex-husband's judgmental attitude and his quickness to point out what he thought were others' problems. This man tried to talk through his concerns about that with him, but my ex wasn't open to trying to understand those concerns or to think he might need to change something. I wanted to be honest. I no longer worried about protecting his image, nor was it just to put him down.

Q: *Why not masturbate to release the stress? I know that the Catholic church is a champion of discouraging women from masturbation. In France, the Catholic church calls masturbation a perversion which can render you deaf.*

A: Once, I came across information about a sex position which I wanted to try. That was the boldest and most assertive I had ever been about sex with him. His response was so squelching that I gave up immediately.

Q: *Do you think there are millions of religious people going through the same reality?*

A: I'm sure that's true. That's why I wanted to make it public. The elders asked me shortly after I wrote my letter if they could suggest another woman at church read it because she was going through similar struggles. Of course, I agreed. She and I talked after she read it and I believe it helped her make progress in her own marriage.

Q: *Do you still believe in abstaining before marriage based on your experience? Did you preach the same to your girls?*

A: Well, I failed in that department. They knew our convictions, but because I never could talk to them about how great sex is after marriage, I just didn't have that talk. I couldn't fake it or be a hypocrite. I knew I didn't want them to experience what I was experiencing, but they knew what the Bible teaches.

Q: *So, now most young people don't believe in abstaining before marriage in America?*

A: There are lots of religions in America, but the fact that my kids' generation has largely given up on church is evidence that they didn't see the real thing lived out in any way that was attractive to them. Our culture has become more and more secular, not shaped by Christian morals as in the past. But, as I've told you before, I have had many disappointments, too, with many of my church experiences, so until I can show my own daughters from my own experience what I know is true and is God's intention for the Christian lifestyle to be like, I'd only be talking from what they'd consider to be theory and not reality. I do think more and more people are longing for more meaningful church experiences than they've found so far, though.

In conclusion, according to a survey done by the French agency Ipsos, French men have an average of 11 sexual partners prior to marrying for the first time and French women have eight. In the U.S., a study done by the University of Utah found that the average number of sexual partners before marrying is ten (Nicholas H. Wolfinger 2016). In the U.S., according to an NBC news survey, in adults aged 20 to 59 women have an average of four sexual partners before marrying for the first time while men have seven.

I am far from being a judge of what is wrong or right in terms of sexuality, but I will say that many men and women in France prefer multiple sexual experiences before they settle down. Others prefer to preserve themselves for their Prince Charming. Sex alone may not be enough to make a great couple, but a sexless marriage is like a car missing a wheel.

Chapter 19

What Does a French Man Consider to Be a

Good Relationship?

"Partager le même lit ne veut pas dire partager le meme rêve."

Sharing the same bed doesn't mean sharing the same dream.

An American friend of mine, curious about all things French, asked how I define a good relationship. It is impossible to speak on behalf of all French men. Defining the word "good" is relative. Taking the time to get to know one another is the key to building a good relationship, in my personal view. Attraction can be sporadic, and I don't believe it is always permanent. There is no medicine to combat aging or the transformation of becoming a mother or father.

We all change with time and experiences. I think that complementary characteristics and compatibility are the key to a good relationship. I wouldn't love a partner who is my clone, a partner who likes the same foods, shows, and movies. Life would be boring. I consider a good relationship one in which there is respect for the differences between the partners. While I have heard many women in America say that men are shallow and do not understand women, I don't think any of us really do. Trying to understand a woman is like trying to understand an equation of multiple unknowns.

I would never claim to understand women, but I do try to see all situations from a woman's perspective before I offer my own.

My idea of a good relationship is being with someone that appreciates my forwardness. The French are known for being direct. If you ask a French man whether he thinks you look good in those pants, be prepared to hear the truth. This directness might seem rude or offensive in other cultures. I would expect my partner to want my true thoughts when she is asking me questions, and I expect the same from her when it is my turn to ask.

One thing that I don't see enough of in America is physical communication such as hugs, snuggling, and holding hands. Not necessarily in the form of PDA, but in private as well. It is what we call in French *câlins*. These are silent ways of expressing love or healing after an argument. Maybe Americans can learn that silence is also a language. Partners in a healthy relationship are not always talking about their past lovers. They are both secure in their current relationship and understand that the touch of your partner, sexual or otherwise, is important.

Love is a beautiful thing but can also be very difficult to keep alive. It is like a campfire in the middle of winter. A good relationship is about "us" without ignoring the "I" and the "you." Everyone can be themselves while together. Keeping that campfire alive requires effort from both partners. I would say that respect is another key factor for a good relationship. All situations can be handled with love and respect.

Sex is like oxygen for me. The frequency of it is important. With that said, I would rather have great sex than sex that becomes a marital duty or a chore. I do not comprehend a sexless relationship unless there is a medical reason. My idea of an ideal relationship is to have two separate bedrooms and two bathrooms in the same home. It gives us both our personal space and privacy for when we need it. I prefer hosting her in my space and she hosts me in her space from time to time. This arrangement will solve issues such as a partner's sensitivity to noise (for the snorers among us) or a partner who loves to read before bedtime. Even a remote control can be a source of an argument. We say in French that familiarity kills respect.

Dinner in France is a form of culinary love making. It is a time to reconnect with your partner over a thoughtful meal and a glass of wine. French dinners are known for lasting well into the evening. For a French couple, dinner becomes an opportunity for romance. In America, dinner seems more of a hurried obligation. Couples do not always eat at the same table, or even in the same room. Although I understand the reality of long workdays and parental obligations, deciding to make every dinner a special occasion can only enhance your day. Bring out your inner French!

Another quality of a good relationship, in my opinion, is having a partner who loves to travel and experience other cultures. A good relationship for me is one in which you occasionally go out to dinner, see a concert, or a comedy show. There should be a good balance between being a homebody and someone who loves to get out for a weekend at the beach or the mountains.

When I am in love, I am involved deeply in the relationship, especially having a partner who reassures you, consoles you, motivates you to go forward. The most important thing is to be happy together.

Be romantic. Write a love letter. Even a brief, hand-written note is enough to show your gratitude to a worthy partner.

Start your day by expressing love and appreciation for your partner. Love will not be proved by how many times you say *Je t'aime* (I love you), but by how you show your love.

A small dose of jealousy does not have to be toxic. It can add spice to a relationship. A husband showing a bit of jealousy is evidence that he loves his wife and is protective of their relationship. This is something to expect if you date a Frenchman.

Chapter 20

Raising Future Women and Being a Soccer Dad

"Les enfants sont comme de l'argile; vous pouvez mouler l'argile pour faire de bonnes ou de mauvaises cruches."

Children are like clay; you can mold the clay to make good or bad jugs.

After my divorce, I found myself playing the role of father and mother to my daughters. Being a single dad has given me the opportunity to really bond with my daughters. I am discovering my strengths and weaknesses. Some days I surprise myself by the degree of patience that I have developed as a single father, while other days I get irritated by the slightest things. Parenting has its challenges, but it is also a joy to discover the personality of each of my daughters. My days off from work are spent chauffeuring the girls from one activity to another. There are times when getting back to work is my first real chance to take a deep breath and reflect. One thing that is clearly observable of girls is their ability to talk.

Without exaggeration, there are times when they can talk one hundred words a minute.

I also notice the same talent for conversation among the women that converge at the activities my girls attend and it all makes perfect sense. Women are mature daughters. Being the father of a son as well, it does puzzle me why girls have not only the desire to communicate but the ability to express themselves so much more than boys. One day I was called to our kitchen over the discovery of an ant. That discovery was followed by extensive conversation.

When my girls are having a disagreement, I give them time to talk things out and resolve their differences without my help. If they can't resolve the problem on their own, I intervene. We then discuss the right thing to do and the reasons why.

Trying to make everyone happy when deciding what's for dinner is another challenge. Putting the decision up to a vote usually leaves us with a tie between chicken and burgers. Rarely will all four of my girls agree on anything. Three may want to go swimming while the fourth one complains that she hates the smell of the chlorine. They plead to be taken to multiple places at once, but, as we say in France, *Le chien a quatres pattes, mais il ne suit qu'une direction* (a dog has four legs but can only go in one direction).

After stories have been read and all four of my daughters are asleep, I take full advantage of the down time to catch up with French television. My seven-year-old daughter is a self-proclaimed morning person. She's not wrong. This little girl is a true human alarm clock. She is at my bedside between 6:00 and 6:15 am, without fail. Once she asked me, "Dad, why do people have to sleep?" I replied, "You need your sleep to have the energy to do everything you have planned for the next day, and I need my sleep to keep up with the four of you."

I have learned the hard way not to make promises using measures of time to a seven-year-old. I remember telling my daughter that we would leave the house in five minutes. She walked away counting out loud. I could hear her reach the number sixty and begin counting all over again. There are days when my body does not respond well to waiting around for extended periods of time when multiple activities take place back-to-back. I will admit that on occasion I allow my imagination to entertain the idea of my two oldest daughters having their driver's licenses and helping me get everyone to their destinations.

Teenage daughters also have a talent for testing a father's patience.

I never know what to expect at the start of their day. When one is in a bad mood, I consider it a fairly good day, but when both my teen daughters are in bad mood, I have learned to give them some space. These are the very same girls who are quick to remind me to watch my language if I curse in French at another driver while stuck in traffic. Jean Jacques Rousseau said, *La patience est amère, mais le fruit est doux* (patience is bitter, but its fruit is sweet). It is beautiful to see my daughters exhibiting tolerance when they interact with other children. My girls don't mention differences in skin color or any other kind of difference; they just see other children.

My grandmother Elizabeth has a philosophy of life that I try to inculcate in my children: "Together you are stronger." Having four daughters means four individual destinies. I hope they will look after each other, united, even as adults. I am determined to raise my daughters to be independent women. I don't want them to grow up with the notion of needing to be rescued by a man. If they choose to be in a healthy relationship out of love and not necessity, then I have done my job.

I can't remember how many times I've forgotten to eat, being distracted by so many activities at once. I often call my older sister in Normandy when I feel I could benefit from some sound parenting advice. Being a parent gives my life a purpose and when my daughters are not at home, my house feels like a desolate graveyard and I miss them dearly. It is my responsibility as a father to shape their character as future women. The strength of a woman starts at her family roots. The deeper the roots, the stronger the tree to withstand the wind. My aunts living their lives in France are very close to each other. In most families in France, sisters are very close. Family is the most important entity in the life of any woman. In a bad relationship or marriage, it is always important to maintain a good relationship with your sisters. The fight for women rights in America also starts inside of the family unit.

I often tell my daughters that my role as father is to facilitate their future, but the unity among them will guarantee solidarity among themselves. United as sisters they will be stronger. What I have seen in America in some families is that an older sister has no say with the younger sisters because her bank account is not as full as those of her siblings. The sister with more wealth rules.

Chapter 21

The Progression of Gender Equality in France

NAPOLEON - KING OF MISOGYNY

"On ne peut pas aimer la pomme et détester le pommier."

You cannot love apples and hate apple trees.

Although this is not a history book, it is important to know how French women have liberated themselves, from the French Revolution to today. Despite his extraordinary imagination and love for his strong-minded mother, Napoleon was also the worst enemy of French women, believing that they were nothing but "baby-making machines."

I will focus on important dates and a few women who pioneered the fight for equality such as Olympe De Gourges (1748-1793). She was an aristocrat who claimed women's rights but was guillotined for standing against the Montagnards (a political group during the French Revolution).

Napoleon passed a law called "Napoleonic Code" in 1804, a civil code that officially confined women in their family. This misogynistic law locked women under the authority of their father or their husband. Married women were treated as minors by their spouses. Here are a few examples of laws under the Napoleonic Code:

- The husband has the right to control, read her letters, and approve her friends.
- Adultery committed by the woman was severely punished by law.
- Women were not allowed to work without the husband's permission (if she worked the husband held her pay).
- Women didn't have to go to high school or college.
- The children from the marriage belonged to the husband.
- The husband was the owner of his wife and children, the way a farmer owns an orchard.

To reinforce his misogyny, two more amendments were added to the civil code in 1810:

- House duties were the responsibility and obligation of women.

- There is no rape between spouses.

In 1816 another amendment banned divorce. In 1848 the first women's magazine was born in France: *La Voix de la Femme* (*The Woman's Voice*).

It is important to mention the suffragettes, a radical group of feminists who claimed equality and used violence to force change. In 1908, a violent repression was organized against them. The French figure of radical feminism and social activism was Madeleine Pelletier (1874-1939), the first female physician in the field of psychiatry in France. She believed that only women should decide if and when to become a mother. She was an advocate for abortion and contraception and believed that heterosexuality was misused to oppress women. She dressed as a man to distance herself from femininity until her death a year after the Napoleonic Code was abolished in 1938, ending women's obedience laws and giving them more rights.

SIMONE VEIL: THE TRUE FRENCH WOMEN'S RIGHTS CHAMPION

"Personne n'arrive a son but sans y employer toutes ses forces."

No one achieves their goal without using all their strength.

The abolishment of the Napoleonic Code gave French women more rights, such as the right to be admitted to a hospital without their husbands' approval and protection from being accused of abandonment by their husbands. It gave them the right to attend college and even own an identification card. But husbands still had the power to decide the location of the family home and were still legally the head of the house. On April 21, 1944, French women obtained the right to vote and effectively voted on April 29, 1945. However, they did not gain the right to work without the husband's permission until 1965 and abortions were illegal until 1970.

The Manifesto of the 343 (*Le Manifeste des 345*) was a petition signed by 345 women that was published on April 5, 1971, in the magazine *Nouvel Observateur*. Each woman who signed claimed openly that she had had an abortion as an act of disobedience. By admitting it publicly, the women were exposed to criminal prosecution. The manifesto called for the legalization of abortion and free access to contraception.

I asked my longtime neighbor, Florence, who was 17 years old in 1971, about this. She said, "It was like thunder. That manifesto paved the way to legalize abortion. Thousands of women were already having them clandestinely."

Simone Veil was the key in lifting French women's rights in the 1970s. She was a Holocaust survivor and a graduate of an elite French law school. Veil worked as a lawyer and a politician, and in 1956 became a magistrate, holding a senior position at the national penitentiary of France. During that tenure, she improved conditions in the women's prison. In 1964, as director of civil affairs, she improved women's rights status, especially dual parenting rights. Prior to this moment, in France children had belonged to their fathers exclusively. From 1974 to 1979, Madam Veil was France's Minister of Health. On December 4, 1974, a law that she had proposed, in favor of easy access to contraception, was passed. She introduced a law that legalized abortion in France; "Loi Veil," named after her, was passed on January 17, 1975.

Simone Veil made these important achievements in a male-dominated senate/assembly. In 1971, the French senate was made up of only 1.4% women (4 out of 284 senators). In 1973, there were only 12 women out of over 490 lawmakers (2.4%).

Obviously, Simone Veil could not have achieved what she did without the support of men. French male lawmakers changed their attitude. In order to advance women's rights, we do not necessarily need the women to outnumber the men. We simply need to have the conscientiousness of the men advanced enough to see increased rights for women as a benefit for all, rather than see it as a threat to the male ego.

France has since created a department that exclusively handles issues between genders. Marlene Schiappa is the Secretary of Equality between men and women. As of 2019, no such position exists in America. As a woman, Schiappa understands the challenges women face in today's society. In 2012, women made up only 12% of French ambassadors around the world. After Schiappa's nomination in 2017, that number rose to 26%. Under Schiappa, a bill was passed to combat sexual violence and street harassment. She also helped raise the age of sexual consent from 13 to 15 years old.

Chapter 22

Domestic Violence

Personne n'est plus arrogant envers les femmes, plus agressif ou meprisant qu'un homme inquiet pour sa virilite. –Simone de Beauvoir

No one is more arrogant toward women, more aggressive or scornful, than the man who is anxious about his virility.

I recall being seven when I witnessed my father beating my mother. At that age I knew something wrong was happening, but as a child I couldn't comprehend it and couldn't stop my father from hitting and kicking my mother. I can recall one specific beating that kept her face swollen and bruised for days. She stayed inside the house, too embarrassed to be seen by our neighbors. The irony is that my mother was the daughter of the police chief. She kept domestic violence a secret from her parents and other family members.

I grew up extremely sensitive to violence against women. My father got away with it and my parents eventually divorced. I have lived both in France and America and it seems to me that violence against women has never taken a holiday. Every day, women are killed or physically harmed by a partner. Women are not drums for men. Reading through statistics on domestic violence that leads to the killing of women by their partner is alarming, both in France and America.

A woman is killed in France every three days by her partner or former partner. France is not a country with a culture of guns like America, making this statistic even more surprising. Violence against women was not a topic in the spotlight, but French women today are more vocal and demanding of action to combat a serious problem. On one hand, French society wants to preserve their reputation for being the country of love and human rights. On the other hand, there is a need for government intervention to help find solutions.

Intimate terrorism is common in the US as well as in France. The statistics of the US National Coalition Against Domestic Violence are clear. Like in France, women are more likely to be killed by a spouse or an ex-lover. I question the motives of these partners. What could move a person to end the life of someone they profess to love? Is it jealousy? Is it anger over being rejected? We are in the twenty first century, and yet there are men who still view women as property. The pattern of violent men is to say *sorry* and beg for forgiveness, which can often include phony crocodile tears, followed by passionate make-up sex. These predators are often forgiven until the next assault. Too often, the opportunity for women to forgive their aggressor ends abruptly. The same pattern of behavior is seen in both France and America.

Many of the women killed in France by a partner have reached out for police protection but were denied it. In some cases, the same woman is found murdered a few weeks later. The reason so many French women are denied protection is due to a ridiculous law that distinguishes between the words violence and danger. In other words, the law states that a woman who is physically abused is not necessarily in danger. French women are fighting to change this law so that violence and danger are synonymous.

In the United States, eighty percent of victims of domestic violence are women. But American women have an advantage that French women do not have.

One difference worth noting is that a woman in America who fears for her life can file for a restraining order and legally obtain a firearm for personal protection. In France, owning a firearm is illegal. French women rely on the police to intervene.

In some cases, the response by the police after an emergency call from the victim is too late. In the last six years, the number of women killed by a partner or former partner has increased. This is one of the few areas of government that the French are struggling to resolve.

There are men who would not consider a slap as a beating, pretending that a slap is not violence. Strangely, when caught, men sometimes blame their fathers for not teaching them to respect women. Violence is an expression, therefore a choice. Violence is a matter of control of emotions. Domestic violence awareness month may help to remind men and women that violence cannot replace words; year-long awareness would be even better. I am aware that some men are victims of domestic violence, too.

What the police in both France and America seem to not get is that it is more important to follow the victims of violence after their complaints. Spain is leading the way in Europe by taking every complaint from women seriously. It is clear that women under the charm and the promises of "it will never happen again" from an abuser tend to drop their complaints. That is the most dangerous phase for her and can lead to her becoming the next statistic. It is not possible to have a policeman behind every female victim of domestic violence, but the early signs of verbal, emotional and physical abuse should not be ignored. It is wise for law enforcement not to allow women to remove a formal complaint made about an abusive partner, simply because he has convinced her to retract the complaint.

I give French women a lot of credit for their ability to organize themselves as collectives and coalitions of family and friends of victims of domestic violence, to put pressure on the government to do something. Their ability to use media to get their message heard is impressive. I believe that workplaces, schools and churches must play a big role in educating men to minimize their chances of becoming perpetrators.

Chapter 23

Abortion Rights In the US

"Quand deux elephants se battent, c'est l'herbe qui souffre."
When two elephants fight, it is the grass that suffers.

The State of Alabama has brought America into the headlines around the world by passing tough laws against abortion. Abortion rights are one of sacred rights for women. I do not believe in abortion; it is never the best solution, but I do believe in the rights for women to choose what is best for them. I reached out to a feminist organization in France to comment on what is going on in Alabama. The news of tough laws against abortion was covered by all the French media. Most of the French feminist movements have condemned that move. I reached out to an association called CADAC (Coordination des Associations pour le Droit a la Contraception et a l'avortement.) for comments, I spoke to Melodie who prefers to give her personal opinion, " I thought the US was more civilized than that. I am realizing that the US is a barbaric country. I couldn't believe what I heard on the news.

No woman aborts by joy, it is always a tough decision no matter the reasons." She asked me why things are different in the US compared to France?

I responded by telling her that the war between conservatives, therefore religious against liberals is a permanent battle in the US, and churches are very influential with lawmakers. As in many States in the US, this move by Alabama's republican senators was a strategic one to contest the legality of abortion in the US adopted in 1973. I also explained to her that as we are approaching the next presidential elections, this controversy will certainly help the actual president of the United States. Melodie asked me why women cannot stand up and go on the streets and protest? Americans do not have a culture of strikes and protests. American women don't speak the same language when it comes to abortion and contraception as in France.

Conservatives don't even accept the idea of a woman's choice to decide if she should or should not keep a baby. I added that I was reading a survey made by the agency ifop in France showing that more than 85% of women are in favor of pro-choice. But also, the majority would prefer to avoid abortion. In the United Stated laws are never permanent.

A law passed in the 70's can still be challenged 50 years later.

The two political parties often challenge the laws that they do not like once in power. Alabama's senators, (all men), sent a message to women in their state and the rest of America that men can still have control of their fecundity. It is simply insane for men to decide on behalf of women. It is part of democracy, too. When pro-abortion women, mostly liberal, fight those against abortion, typically conservative, it is like when two elephants fight, it is the grass that suffers. At the end of the day women are the biggest losers.

Chapter 24

MEETING FRANCE

C'est dans la connaissance des conditions authentiques de notre vie qu'il nous faut puiser la force de vivre et des raisons d'agir. - **Simone de Beauvoir**

It is in knowing the authentic conditions of our life that we must draw the strength to live and the reasons for acting.

Sometimes, it is better to be alone than to be in bad company. This attitude is valid in any culture. While living in Moirans, near Grenoble in France, in my twenties, I never met a man or woman who didn't want or hope to find a good partner to have a great relationship with. In general, French men only feel complete if we have a woman in our lives. I also recognize that men in France are dominant in a relationship. This tendency to always want to be in control, without giving space, voice and respect to our partner is certainly causing more trouble for men. I have seen similarities in America. More and more women are fed up with the culture of a woman who needs a man to be happy in her life.

I met Frances through a common friend. Knowing that I was writing a book to American women, my friend insisted that I speak with Frances because she is her inspiration. Frances is the definition of a strong and independent American woman. Frances is the President and CEO of a healthcare organization in North Carolina. It took me two days to think about how to formulate my request for a conversation with her in the form of an interview. Eventually, I sent her a message. I was flattered by her acceptance. Frances agreed to meet with me upon returning from a vacation to Paris. I drove to meet her at her office in the town of Raleigh, in North Carolina. Frances saw me parking my car, walked to the door, and held it open for me saying, "Come in." She is beautiful, charismatic, and carries herself with elegance. Frances has a demeanor about her that is unmistakably French. She offered me something to drink and sat on her chair facing me and said, "I read the overview of your book. I like what I read and I think it will help your daughters in the future." I was flattered and I couldn't wait to hear her responses to my questions.

Q: *Who is Frances?*

A: I grew up in the town of Swannanoa near Asheville and the town of Black Mountain in the Western part of North Carolina. I got married when I was 16 and I got divorced when I was 21. I never thought of marrying again. I raised two children by myself, educated myself, worked all the time while I was getting my education and never looked back. I never expected anything from anyone. I raised my only daughter with a mindset of never depending on a man, your mother, your grandparents or inheritance, or anything. My message to my daughter is that you must be strong within yourself, be able to provide and secure your future.

Q: *Where did you get that mindset?*

A: I think I got it from my mother who was of a different generation. We were raised in the country and even though we were very poor, my mother was self-sufficient. My mother stayed married to my father for 60 years while working two jobs. I think she influenced me.

Q: *Do you associate with like-minded women?*

A: Yes, reflecting on my friendships, I can say that the majority of the women I know are like me. I choose strong-minded women as friends.

Q: *How old is your daughter and does she think like you?*
A: My daughter is 47 and strong-willed. I raised her to be a strong, independent woman.

Q: *Why did you decide not to marry again?*
A: The main reason is that I married too early. Living in the country, marrying at a young age was normal. My mother married at age 12.

Q: *Do you have siblings?*
A: Yes, I have four and I am the second oldest. I took care of them as well while my mother was working two jobs and my father worked in a factory. When I look back, I realize how well my parents did without going to college. We were never hungry, no fine car, no fine house, but we were all together. When the textile mill came to town, all of us worked in that mill. My dad said to me, "You will go to college." My dad had a third-grade education, he was poor, and he didn't have the opportunity to better himself, but he

insisted that I better myself. The experience of working in a textile mill reinforced my determination to do better in life.

Q: *What did you learn from your father?*
A: My father was a functioning alcoholic. I was my father's favorite. He is the main reason that I got married so young. I wanted to get away from the drinking. At some point he had his driver license suspended for drinking and driving. Luckily, we lived a mile from the factory, so he walked every morning to work. Because of my father, I knew the difference between moonshine and liquor store alcohol. I did get my work ethics from both my father and mother.

Every Friday in the afternoon, we all loaded into his station wagon and drove 15 miles to the grocery store. My mom would take all five of her children to the grocery store while my father would go across the street to the liquor store. Even so, my father was a hard worker, no matter what.

Q: *What do you think of the #Metoo movement?*
A: I can't imagine that all these actresses allowed somebody to touch them and not say anything about it. I have trouble comprehending it. I have mixed feelings about it.

Q: *During your career you never faced sexism?*

A: My superior at that time, in a mostly male dominated field, looked at my records as director of a nursing home and took a chance on me, a divorced mother of two infants. I can say that the company was supportive of me. They put me in an administrator training program.

When I became a director at a nursing home, I wanted to apply for a position as an administrator in one the largest chains of nursing homes in the United States. I asked them to have confidence enough in me to become an administrator. I told them that I can run operations as well as any man. When I was applying and talking to my superiors no one showed confidence in me. The director of operations looked at me and said, "Fran, we know you are a good nurse, but do you know anything about numbers? Do you know how to run a business? Do you know finance? Do you know a PNL?" I told them, if you let me have the staff and resources that I need, I can do that job. I told them that I have a degree in Science, and I took trigonometry and chemistry, so I am capable of working with numbers.

[Frances did not directly say that she faced sexism, but the line of questioning that she received when she applied for the administrator position was obviously sexist.]

Q: *Still you never thought of marrying?*

A: I never allowed anybody to come too close to me. My ex-husband married a younger woman. He never had a close relationship with my children. But he is a good person. I walked away from my marriage. When you married that young, he was a nice person but as I grew and matured, he was not the person that I wanted to be with.

Marrying or dating was never my priority; I had things that I wanted to do. My biggest thing was my children. I didn't want anybody else telling them what to do, I didn't want to share them with anybody, I wanted to be the person who makes the decision for their education. I never trusted anybody. I had relationships but I never look anything outside of it.

Q: *Certainly, some men wanted to marry you?*

A: Yes, every time I ended the relationship first. The person that I cared for the most was younger than me. He never married and never had children. When I saw him getting serious about us, I ended it. I didn't want to have more children and his mother was against the relationship because of our age difference. In all my relationships, I always put myself in the position of being in control. But with this particular man, I thought I was losing control, so I chose to walk away.

The last physical relationship that I had was 35 years ago. I was 35 years old. Don't get me wrong, people used to flirt with me. I just have this wall. I just have this persona. I don't want a man in my home who will say that I put my toothbrush in the wrong place or that I left my underwear on the floor. It was my plan to be where I am today. I want to be left alone. My daughter's life experience is different, she doesn't agree with me. She doesn't want to be alone.

Q: *Don't you want to feel loved?*
A: I can honestly say no. Not a man, not a woman. I don't desire anybody. I love my life. I am financially secure, I retired twice, I love going out shopping and I am perfectly happy.

Q: *Do you think that you are successful today because you didn't want a man in your life?*

A: You are absolutely right!

Q: *What is your biggest regret?*

A: My biggest regret is not spending more time with my children when they were younger.

Q: *Do you have any dreams or goals left to fulfill?*

A: As President and CEO of this organization, I want it to grow more and I want to spend more time with my family.

My thoughts about the interview:

Frances has proven that education is the key to fighting poverty. I would also add that the education of women is the key to fighting sexism and disrupting men's psychological attitude of feeling superior to women. Frances is a self-made success, going from poverty to becoming one of the top experts in her field.

She stunned me many times during this interview. Frances was not shy about saying that she has not had a sexual relationship in over thirty-five years. She strongly believes that taking the focus away from relationships and placing it on her career has been a major reason for her success. Frances was quick to point out that she has no regrets regarding her decision to stay away from men. I asked her if she had relationships with other women instead. Frances assured me that she is heterosexual, but she willingly guarded herself from romance.

She never left her children while bettering herself. Honestly, I believe she made the right decision. I see it as a necessary sacrifice. She did it all alone even though she described her ex-husband as a "good person" but never mentioned if he played his role as a parent. Men should realize that they are still parents after divorce.

When she showed her mixed feelings about the #Metoo movement, she reminded me of the reaction of the French legendary actress Brigitte Bardot, who sees the movement as a witch hunt against men. I personally don't believe that the intent of the #Metoo movement is to hurt men, but to demand respect. The idea that a woman needs a man to succeed in life is obsolete. Today, women have options if they want children without being in a relationship with a man. I am impressed by Frances' unwillingness to compromise on her goals. This is something I do not see enough of among American women compared to French women. Frances reminds me of Sonia, who is a close family friend. She lives in the suburb of Paris in the town of Pontault Combault. Sonia has chosen to have an occasional mate "based on my mood" but mostly she prefers to satisfy her sexual needs by herself. As she put it, "it is easier than dealing with the stress of a relationship with a man."

Chapter 25

Makeup and Self Image

Le sourire est le plus beau maquillage qu'une femme puisse porter
A smile is the most beautiful makeup a woman can wear.

We live in a period where many people define themselves based on their image. Sitting in Cafe la Fourmiliere in Lyon, France, drinking a cold beer, watching people walk by, I barely notice the women wearing makeup. I asked a few men how they feel about it as I am used to seeing makeup frequently worn by American women.

Emmanuel in his 50's remarked, "Makeup that accentuates a woman's beauty is discreet. Too much make up is annoying."

Julien, in his 30's added, "Light makeup is fine, if it can hide small imperfections." Driving in the cities of America, I am often surprised to see how many times women are doing their makeup while driving or at the stop light, especially during the early morning rush hour. The "sorry for not wearing makeup" coming from a woman often catches me off guard. My curiosity pushed me to ask a woman colleague at work, if it is something required or expected in the American culture.

Kimberly said, "We feel like we're being rated daily based on our looks. That is our motivation to give up an extra 30 minutes of sleep every morning and spend that time applying makeup."

Jacqueline said, "I think of makeup as an accessory, like jewelry. It makes me feel confident and ready to face the world. I don't wear it to please anyone other than myself." I know for sure that French women love their mascara, but many avoid the additional products. Going natural in France is a popular decision. It seems the consensus is that women wear makeup to feel great in their skin, to feel pretty. Makeup should not be a requirement to be successful in love or at work. French men do not expect women to wear makeup on a date, at least not among my circle. Most of the time, French men do not even notice it, at least I don't. Nicely polished fingernails, however, I do notice. Makeup doesn't define femininity in France. We respect a woman's freedom to choose what makes her feel great in her own skin. I do not believe that makeup is necessary to hide imperfections either. A woman, American or French is most beautiful when she does not appear aware of her own beauty.

Chapter 26

How I See It: Conclusion

I wrote this book with no intention of being a preacher, nor to create a diatribe, but as a man who has lived in both France and America and who is the father of daughters. I thought of writing this book five years ago after meeting many women, married and single, who shared their stories with me. I have also spent two decades observing interactions between American women and their partners.

My motivation in writing this book is to help American women wake up to the reality of their plight - living in a society that only pays lip service to equal rights for women - and use their minds, strength and power to demand change. We need equality between men and women to make a better world. I am pointing out what French women are achieving by pressing their government to make women's rights a priority in France. In fact, the French government has a secretary of state in charge of equality between men and women. While French women are still fighting stereotypes, sexism, and sexual harassment on a daily basis, they are also demanding equal pay and speaking out against domestic violence.

I believe that American women are not fighting hard enough. If things are not moving fast enough, American women should change their strategy to force the change.

I challenge American women to *"Vive la Différence,"* to follow the example of French women by making equal rights for women in America a priority. I am closing this book with a letter to you.

Dear American Women,

Writing this book has been a personal labor of love for me, dedicated to the most important women in my life on two continents. For my strong and fearless French sister, aunts, mother, and grandmother: I thank you for being such positive female role models and showing me by example how a woman should be treated. You are the inspiration for the essays and reflections in this book.

For my four beautiful daughters here in America, and for all American women: I hope that the most important lesson you learn from your French counterparts is that you have the power to make changes and you don't have to accept the status quo.

In the realm of love, I am doing my very best to teach my daughters what smart French women know before investing their hearts into a relationship. Your choice of partners will affect your destiny. Love can bring us great happiness if we choose wisely and not allow our sense of self to become lost in the relationship. I hope that American women will understand my philosophy of love. To love is to give a person the power to destroy you. You're handing over the remote control to your life. Your partner can either nurture that love or tear it down. There is nothing wrong with following your heart when selecting a partner, but don't exclude your brain from the process - that's what I tell my daughters. Choose wisely, give it your all, and allow yourself permission to walk away if it doesn't work. Don't compromise your values or your integrity for any reason.

I hope that after sharing my perspective and learning from enlightened French women, you will raise your expectations of men and hold them accountable for their actions. Be clear, precise and intentional about your needs, wants, and goals.

I applaud American men who are willing to join the fight for equality between men and women. They understand the struggles that women endure every day in a misogynistic society. As French President Macron stated, "Equality between men and women is absolutely a fundamental subject of the vitality of our society, our economy, and our democracy."

I want to remind you, American women, that you have a collective voice. There is power in numbers. Just like your French sisters, you can spark change by demanding equal rights for women. I ask that you put aside political differences and find candidates at the local, regional, and national levels who can elevate your agenda for women's rights. I see American women, liberal and conservative, disagreeing and losing sight of the true focus. It is like two lungs within the same body forgetting that they have the same goal. Vote out individuals who perpetuate sexist viewpoints and disrespect women. Demand justice for women who are victims of sexual violence and gender discrimination. Insist on the rights of immigrant women to keep their children. Make equal pay for equal work a priority. Seek out like-minded women who are opposed to a board of directors that is primarily male. If you can't find a representative who is passionate about women's rights, run for office and become that change. I have seen your priceless contributions in all sectors of life - economic, political, artistic, cultural, and social. Your capabilities are boundless.

"Une vraie femme, c'est celle qui sait défendre sa dignité."

A true woman is one who knows how to defend her dignity.

Made in the USA
Las Vegas, NV
30 March 2023

69910502R00095